PRAISE FOR *US*
ARTIFICIAL INTELLI...
IN MARKETING

'Katie King has a fantastic way of captivating her audience and ensuring the reader is both aware of and excited about the role AI has to play in our personal and professional futures. This book, and the introduction of the Scorecard into marketers' lives, will be invaluable in setting brands up for success as they shift to a world where AI must be at the centre of marketing strategy.' **Thom Nowell, Football Brand Manager, Nike UK**

'An inspirational book in the third millennium of communications. A highly recommended read for those curious about the impact of artificial intelligence on marketing and communications.' **Somayeh Heydarali, Internal Communications and Media Relations Supervisor, Nestlé Iran**

'AI and machine learning are already redefining marketing, both within corporates and the agency world – and we're only just starting to understand their potential. My advice, read this book and stay ahead of the curve. A lot has been written about the IoT, big data, cloud computing and robotics – but AI is set to rule them all. If you're in marketing or PR you need to read this book, as AI is set to change the face of both professions for good.' **James Delves, Head of PR and Engagement, The Chartered Institute of Marketing (CIM)**

'The impact of AI in the built environment has been much discussed and analysed. This essential book brings clarity and insight to these conversations and is presented in an accessible way, using real examples that address many misconceptions.' **Paul Bagust, Global Property Standards Director, The Royal Institution of Chartered Surveyors (RICS)**

'Decision-makers will understand that technology does not compete with the human mind – it provides new insight – and this well-researched book offers CEOs and CMOs a deep dive into how to use AI for real and measurable business results.' **Olivier Novasque, CEO, Sidetrade**

'AI has arrived in marketing, there are no brake pads and no reversing. The problem being that there are many people talking about it but few practitioners doing it. King offers a great introduction to the newcomer, as well as a practical guide to the current AI in marketing state of the nation. This is a must-read for the modern marketer.' **Tim Hughes, CEO and Co-founder, Digital Leadership Associates**

'Artificial intelligence is being hailed as the 4th industrial revolution. This important book is essential for anyone in business or marketing wishing to be prepared for the coming of AI.' **Jim Al-Khalili OBE FRS, Professor of Physics; Surrey Professor of the Public Engagement in Science; President, British Science Association**

'Katie King has written a stimulating book that inspires thinking about AI. From personal to marketing and business perspectives, the implications of AI and its potential are engagingly explored.' **Professor Len Tiu Wright, Editor-in-Chief,** *Cogent Business & Management;* **Emeritus Professor, De Montfort University, UK; formerly Professor of Marketing, Huddersfield University, UK**

'Katie King's book is an essential companion to everyone in marketing, from serious students and ambitious young starters through to marketing professionals in agencies and clients, or the most senior marketing directors of large companies. This is not the wave of the future but the wave of the present, benefiting some, making their marketing easier, threatening others and questioning their roles. The key message is, "Don't be an ostrich – get started". This text shows how.' **Merlin Stone, Professor of Marketing and Strategy, St Mary's University, UK**

Using Artificial Intelligence in Marketing

How to harness AI and maintain the competitive edge

Katie King

Publisher's note

Every possible effort has been made to ensure that the information contained in this book is accurate at the time of going to press, and the publisher and authors cannot accept responsibility for any errors or omissions, however caused. No responsibility for loss or damage occasioned to any person acting, or refraining from action, as a result of the material in this publication can be accepted by the editor, the publisher or any of the authors.

First published in Great Britain and the United States in 2019 by Kogan Page Limited.

2nd Floor, 45 Gee Street	c/o Martin P Hill Consulting	4737/23 Ansari Road
London EC1V 3RS	122 W 27th St, 10th Floor	Daryaganj
United Kingdom	New York NY 10001	New Delhi 110002
www.koganpage.com	USA	India

© Katie King, 2019

The right of Katie King to be identified as the author of this work has been asserted by her in accordance with the Copyright, Designs and Patents Act 1988.

ISBNs

HARDBACK	978 0 7494 9797 2
PAPERBACK	978 0 7494 8339 5
E-ISBN	978 0 7494 8340 1

British Library Cataloguing-in-Publication Data

A CIP record for this book is available from the British Library.

Library of Congress Cataloging-in-Publication Data
Names: King, Katie, 1967- author.
Title: Using artificial intelligence in marketing : how to harness AI and maintain the competitive edge / Katie King.
Description: 1st Edition. | New York : Kogan Page Ltd, [2019] | Includes bibliographical references and index.
Identifiers: LCCN 2018050071 (print) | LCCN 2018055771 (ebook) | ISBN 9780749483401 (ebook) | ISBN 9780749483395 (alk. paper) | ISBN 9780749483401 (ebk)
Subjects: LCSH: Marketing–Technological innovations. | Artificial intelligence.
Classification: LCC HF5415.1265 (ebook) | LCC HF5415.1265.K56 2019 (print) | DDC 658.800285/63–dc23

Typeset by Integra Software Services Pvt. Ltd., Pondicherry
Print production managed by Jellyfish
Printed and bound by CPI Group (UK) Ltd, Croydon, CR0 4YY

*To my loving dad Stan, for our inspiring trips
to the Tottenham Swap Shop (where you could exchange
and barter goods) in the 1970s, which fed my insatiable
appetite for books.*

CONTENTS

ABOUT THE AUTHOR

Katie King is a leading business transformation consultant, with a consultancy career spanning 29 years. Katie is an accomplished entrepreneur, trainer and Keynote speaker. She is a frequent commentator on BBC TV and radio, and has delivered two TEDx presentations.

During her career, Katie has advised and trained many of the world's leading global brands including Sky, O2, Virgin, NatWest, Alcatel, Huawei and many more. Katie is CEO of digital marketing agency Zoodikers, and a boutique management consultancy called AI in Marketing. She is also the Co-Founder of AI in FM.

She has an MBA and a degree in languages, as well as a Diploma in Marketing. Katie is married with two children and lives in the UK.

ACKNOWLEDGEMENTS

To my wonderful book publisher, Kogan Page. You brought my book to life and made my dreams come true. After three decades in marketing, ghosting copy for clients, I am elated to be a published author.

Thank you to all my clients, past and present, and to the wonderful contributors to this book. Without your invaluable knowledge, this book would be far less comprehensive, credible and relevant.

To my daughter Scarlett King, who until the eleventh hour, has been a trusted soundboard and editorial assistant.

The foundation of my work ethic hails from my parents Kath and Stan, who, despite limited means, showered me with love but most importantly, taught me self-esteem and belief, and set the bar incredibly high in terms of diligence and fairness.

To my husband Terry and younger daughter Christina, for their patience and support, whilst life was temporarily on hold.

To Chris Hoar, my friend and Co-Founder of AI in FM, who first guided me down the AI path some years back.

The AI wake-up call 01

The strategic transition of marketing

In this opening chapter, we whet the reader's appetite by providing a flavour of the rich content that will unfold over the coming chapters. We first establish what artificial intelligence (AI) actually is and then delve deeply into the role it plays in supporting the marketing function. With insights from leading academics, futurists, analysts and tech disruptors, we consider the very real impact of affordable and accessible AI tools in marketing globally. We analyse the power of a data-driven approach to marketing decision-making and consider how such automation can free up valuable executive time. Let's begin by setting AI into context and first understanding exactly what we mean by it. *The Oxford English Dictionary* gives this definition: 'The theory and development of computer systems able to perform tasks normally requiring human intelligence, such as visual perception, speech recognition, decision-making, and translation between languages' (Oxfordreference.com). Put simply, AI, sometimes referred to as machine learning, denotes the machine's ability to exhibit intelligent behaviour equivalent to, or indistinguishable from, that of a human.

But AI is not as simple as that to classify, as Professor Michael Luck, Dean of Faculty, Natural and Mathematical Sciences, King's College London explains:

> AI is not a single technology. We too often talk about it as if it is. AI is a field; it's a whole band of different technologies, some of which are really quite mature now. It's from those that we've seen some reasonable successes in the media. But some techniques are not so mature; some are new, some still need a lot of work. There is an awful lot that some of the

techniques can do for businesses today. But there is an awful lot more that can be done but we don't yet have the understanding of it. We are still far behind the technical understanding. We have a lack of maturity and a certain naivety in our understanding of what these technologies will enable. There is no single bag of tricks available to be used for all purposes. It is not a silver bullet to everything. The power of AI has been realized; the ability to do certain things much more easily and quickly. But it's just the tip of the iceberg, and if we focus only on those techniques it will be problematic for us.

Dispelling AI myths

Very few advances are causing as much excitement and attention today as AI, and mostly for good reason, as the potential for AI to transform our lives is unprecedented. But with anything new there is motivation for sceptics and headline hungry characters alike to spread fear and misconceptions that more often than not we see spiral out of control.

Max Tegmark, in his book *Life 3.0*, explores some of the basic misconceptions and popular mistruths that often come up when the subject of superintelligent AI is discussed, as well as reasons why you shouldn't buy into them (Figure 1.1).

No brakes; no reversing

AI has exploded into our personal and business lives since 2016 and is now the defining technology of our age. AI is a transformative force, and the pace of change is breathtaking and perpetual. The AI engine is speeding along, with no brakes and no ability to reverse. Intelligent machines can be found in shopping precincts, hospitals and on motorways. This new wave of automation will transform our lives, which is why it has been described as the fourth industrial revolution, following the mechanization of the textile industry, the automation of factories and digitization. The impact of AI on health-care will be immense and will touch all of our lives. An excellent

Figure 1.1 Common myths about superintelligent AI

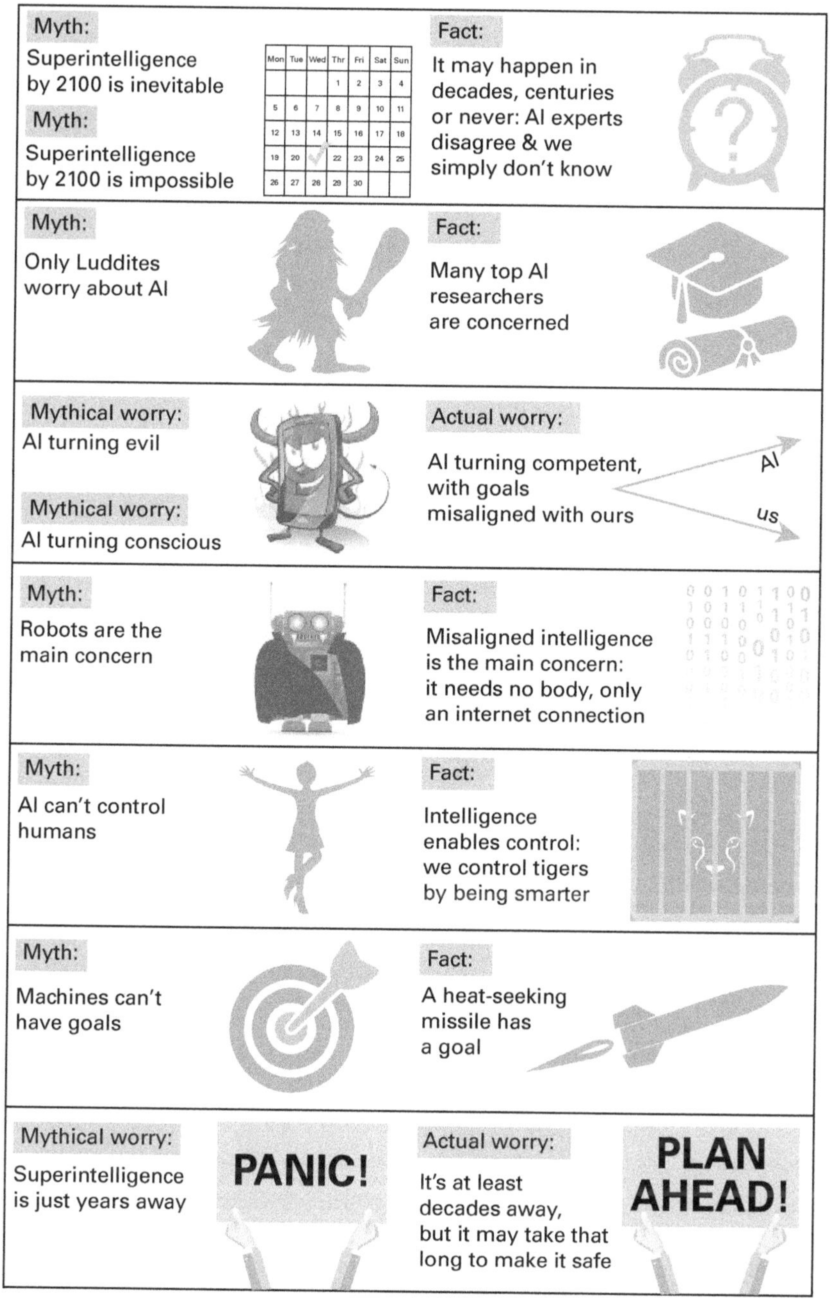
Myth:
Superintelligence by 2100 is inevitable
Myth:
Superintelligence by 2100 is impossible
Mon Tue Wed Thr Fri Sat Sun
Fact:
It may happen in decades, centuries or never: AI experts disagree & we simply don't know
?
Myth:
Only Luddites worry about AI
Fact:
Many top AI researchers are concerned
Mythical worry:
AI turning evil
Mythical worry:
AI turning conscious
Actual worry:
AI turning competent, with goals misaligned with ours
AI
us
Myth:
Robots are the main concern
Fact:
Misaligned intelligence is the main concern: it needs no body, only an internet connection
Myth:
AI can't control humans
Fact:
Intelligence enables control: we control tigers by being smarter
Myth:
Machines can't have goals
Fact:
A heat-seeking missile has a goal
Mythical worry:
Superintelligence is just years away
PANIC!
Actual worry:
It's at least decades away, but it may take that long to make it safe
PLAN AHEAD!

recent example of this can be found in Japan, where AI has successfully identified early stage stomach cancer with a high accuracy rate:

> The breakthrough may help extend the lives of patients in Japan, where stomach cancer is one of the leading causes of death. According to Riken and the National Cancer Center, it took AI only 0.004 seconds to judge whether an endoscopic image showed early stage cancer or normal stomach tissue. AI correctly detected cancer in 80 percent of cancer images, while the accuracy rate was 95 percent for normal tissue. The accuracy rates were as high as those of veteran doctors.
>
> (*The Japan Times*, 2018)

AI: friend or foe for the marketer?

It is an exciting and daunting era to live and work in, and as marketing professionals, we play a leading role. AI and machine learning are redefining marketing and the role of the marketing functions both within companies and in the agency world. As a business function, marketing is further along the curve than others. It certainly is a confusing picture for any CMO, with one credible report contradicting the next with regard to AI's adoption in marketing. Gartner's hype cycle states that AI won't become mainstream for another 5 to 10 years and that, today, we're only at a mere 3 per cent. Econsultancy's research conducted with IBM Watson, which surveyed 1,200 senior marketers, predicts a 29 per cent adoption in 18 months (Econsultancy, 2018). What is undisputed is that whatever country you work in, whatever your sector or size of organization, AI will impact your marketing function fundamentally, if not today, then most certainly in the near to medium term.

For confirmation of this, we have taken the advice of many of the world's leading academics, analysts and brands across multiple industry sectors, as well as a host of technology disruptors. But our job is not to force you into opening your shopping bag to make an impulse AI purchase. Whether you have been mandated to review AI's impact on marketing, our intention is to stretch your mind, to take you outside your comfort zone and then to supply you with a pragmatic framework for success that can be applied to any country and any sector.

Redefining creativity and increasing agility

A recent seminar by McKinsey and Company 'Redefining Creativity in the Data Driven Age' has hit the mark on what incorporating AI means for marketing organizations in a data-driven, agile era (YesICannes, 2018). The seminar was led by Brian Gregg, co-leader of McKinsey's Marketing Service Line within North America and the Retail/Consumer sector on the West Coast, and Jason Heller, Partner and global lead of the digital marketing operations and technology practice at McKinsey and Company. The conclusion was that marketing organizations that optimistically foster AI have the potential to double their return on investment (ROI). Research by McKinsey has unveiled that incorporating data and analytics into the creative process ultimately enhances the customer experience and can double revenue growth. With the rapid pace of technological changes, Gregg and Heller believe that the recipe for growth for marketing organizations in this era involves three key ingredients: 1) to integrate data and creativity; 2) to be agile; and 3) to hire whole-brained talents who can be both creative and rational (YesICannes, 2018).

Some may argue this is easier said than done. Despite the obvious advantages that CMOs can reap from welcoming AI into their organization, many cannot escape the fog of uncertainty. A recent insight from McKinsey and Company has revealed that disruptions are sweeping industries as a result of new technologies and are forcing new business models. Furthermore, these rapid dynamic changes are shaking the confidence of CMOs. Despite perhaps being an expert in your industry, it does not follow that you will be an expert in the complex nature of the new agendas that AI is triggering. The solution? Disruptive times call for increased agility so that leaders can steer their organizations out of the fog of uncertainty. In order to 'do' agile, you must become more agile. This requires greater self-awareness and openness. This new behaviour makes dealing with complexity feel simpler, as the saying goes, 'it pays to make the habit your friend' (Lavoie and Riese, 2018).

Continuous learning

Over the coming years, machines and AI-embedded tools will complement the role that marketing professionals and their co-workers perform. While work will be available, adjustment will be essential, and continuous training and acquiring of new skills will be a focus for all generations in the workplace. This is echoed by Ambrish Bansal, CEO at Klaspad PLC. This is a company whose mission is to be a global leader in immersive yet affordable education. He explains:

> AI and Blockchain are two technologies that may redesign the entire technological (and human) paradigm. AI and Blockchain will make marketing and education hyper individualized. AI will lead to offers being more focussed with increased understanding of individual needs. This will lead to a whole new concept of marketing using AI and complete understanding of consumer psychology and behaviour. The messaging will not only be accurate but also timely, giving better results. With nearly 30 per cent of jobs at risk by 2030 due to automation the workers will need to change their skill set to meet the new challenges. We believe, as do some of our more enlightened education partners, that the skills and the knowledge gained while working should also be educationally recognized. This is already being done using AI and Blockchain micro credits. Life-long learning is the key word in these fast changing times.

AI heatwave

As our impressive array of case studies will illustrate in the impending chapters, AI has weathered decades of winter storms and frozen inactivity, and has entered the dizzy heights of summer. AI or robotic systems can be found in almost every corner of our economy as it stands. AI even permeates cancer detection techniques, as recent research has suggested that AI is more capable of diagnosing cancerous skin lesions than doctors and dermatologists.

An extraordinary case of the medical application of robotics has also recently been announced, praising a group of neurosurgeons at the University of Pennsylvania School of Medicine, USA, who have carried out the first robot-assisted spinal surgery, using cutting-edge robotic arms to remove a tumour from a 27-year-old patient through his mouth.

Robots and automation also feature in the construction industry where a robot named the Semi-Automated Mason (SAM) can lay up to 1,200 bricks a day, compared to 300 to 500 that a human bricklayer is capable of. At the other end of the spectrum, we witness the arrival of a strawberry-picking robot, aiming to fill the short supply of migrant labour in several countries, by using a robot to harvest this highly in demand fruit. And let's not forget the triumph of the AI chatbot industry. Despite being around since the early 1960s, AI has recently taken the online shopping sector by storm as leading retailers are now employing machine-learning algorithms to learn customers' preferences and offer personal recommendations.

AI is undoubtedly creeping in on us from every angle, and its capabilities are ever growing. The extent to which it will impact our economy is unveiled in a recent report by PwC. The report reveals that AI will create as many jobs as it will displace by boosting economic growth over the next 20 years. In absolute terms, the report predicts that around 7 million jobs could be displaced across several industries, but around 7.2 million could be created, giving the UK a net jobs boost of around 0.2 million. The most positive effect is seen in the health and social work sector, where employment could increase by nearly 1 million, equivalent to 20 per cent of existing jobs in the sector (PwC, 2018a).

Epochal change

The impending influx of AI and its impact on our economy have not gone unnoticed. Greg Clark MP, The Secretary of State for Business, Energy and Industrial Strategy in the UK, states:

> The changes that AI is bringing are epochal. There aren't many moments in human history when a technology turns up that changes everything. Agriculture, the wheel, the printing press, then steam,

chemicals, oil, electricity; then the micro-processor. And we are living through one of those moments now. In 2017, when the London-based DeepMind beat Ke Jie, humanity's best Go player, a symbolic date entered the history books. So why is AI quite so revolutionary? Because previous technological revolutions discovered specific ways to improve human lives; this revolution has discovered automatic ways of discovering more. Thus the power to improve the lot of humanity is unprecedented.

Marketing's new Holy Grail

The scale of this technology's abilities to elicit immense change is reinforced by Microsoft co-founder and philanthropist Bill Gates, who clearly believes that AI has tremendous power: 'Certainly it's the most exciting thing going on… It's the holy grail, it's the big dream that anybody who's ever been in computer science has been thinking about' (Ha, 2018). Endorsing this rationale is Professor Michael Luck, Dean of Faculty, Natural and Mathematical Sciences, at King's College London:

> AI has been around for a very long time. I have been working in AI for close to 30 years. We are now, this past few years, in a situation in which AI is suddenly significant and popular and it is no longer inappropriate to talk about. For some time, AI was not something that sold; it was something people didn't really want to be talking about because it wasn't seen to be something that brought with it value in the eyes of the customer. There has been a change in recent years and that change is down to 2 things. One is data – we have an awful lot more than we ever had. The second is that we have a lot more computing power. The combination of those two things has meant that a certain group of techniques of AI have become much more successful, much more capable and have delivered some really significant results for a particular class of applications.
>
> Those are data driven methods, data driven AI techniques for example deep learning and neutral networks, primarily those things which are informed by the data. When you have sufficient quantities,

you can learn things from that and recognize certain things; previously this was not possible. That is the profound change that we have today. But this is one particular set of techniques. It's about recognizing patterns; we see that with voice recognition. It can help us to understand sales and marketing data, looking for trends; looking at patterns of customers to make loan decisions.

Joined up thinking

Professor Luck draws upon AI tools out there today, arguing that they are not in fact as mind-blowing and beneficial as they have the potential to be. In order to truly reap the benefits of the AI techniques many are developing for business purposes – take chatbots for example – we must make use of a combination of substantial and dynamic AI techniques that exist out there today. Professor Luck states:

> There is a real lack of understanding of what these new technologies bring. There has been a lot of hype; they have been doing fantastic things but they are narrow and limited. There is not enough understanding of how they are suited to different kinds of problems.
>
> One example is chatbots; most are quite simple things. They do simple analysis of text and they come back with appropriate responses. They make use of techniques for pattern recognition for example. But the reasoning underneath it is not very deep. It's a simple retrieval of a stock of answers; it's not deep reasoning and as a result many of us can get quite frustrated when we use them. The opportunity there is to put together the basic chatbot component with some more substantial AI techniques that can actually engage in a more substantial dialogue with a human. For example, there is an area of AI called argumentation; it gets computers to argue with others or with humans. It's about understanding when one argument cuts another. If you want a chatbot to be successful in a way that has some more substantial interaction with a human, then you need to do more than we're doing at the moment. You need more logical reasoning; more substantial symbolic AI techniques to be able to engage with the human in the appropriate

terms. It requires the combination of techniques with a whole range of other techniques, which exist, which can do that.

Gartner: the demand for AI

Next we turn to Gartner, Inc., a leading global research and advisory company that helps business leaders across all major functions in every industry and enterprise size with the objective insights they need to make the right decisions. The Gartner Magic Quadrant is regarded as the gold standard for the market position of a technology provider. This applies to both start-ups and established players.

We spoke to Mike J. Walker, who is Vice President, Technology Innovation and Enterprise Architecture Research at Gartner. Walker refers to a flurry of tech innovation, the like of which we have not seen since the post World War Two period of the 1940s. That was a time when net new businesses such as telecoms and transportation expanded on the foundations created during the industrial revolution. Walker predicts that 80 per cent of all emerging technologies will have AI foundations that will span nearly all industries and enable countless business scenarios. These span customer engagement, digital production, smart cities, self-driving cars, risk management, computer vision, and language and speech recognition.

Low barriers to entry

Generally, all industries can adopt AI relatively equally due to the low barriers to entry. The biggest inhibitors to organizations and industries are threefold:

1 The constraints they put on themselves.

2 Organizational readiness. Up to half of all organizations by 2020 will not have the requisite skills in AI and data science skills.

3 Ability to think of innovative business designs/models.

Walker explains:

> Organizations that fail to apply AI will inevitably fall behind rivals that do. Industry leaders such as Alibaba Group, Amazon, Baidu, Facebook and Google view AI as essential to future business success. They use AI as the cornerstone of every new business strategy. Furthermore, Gartner client inquiries about AI have increased by 500 per cent from 2015 to 2017.

The three most often-cited application categories are all related to customer interactions:

1 One in three of the organizations Gartner surveyed said they will link AI to customer engagement applications.
2 Three in 10 said they will integrate AI to call centre service and support.
3 One in four said they will integrate it to digital marketing.

The Gartner Hype Cycle

The Gartner Hype Cycle (Figure 1.2) looks at technologies that show promise in delivering a high degree of competitive advantage. It is aimed at helping leaders to explore and ideate mega-trends to understand the future impacts to their business. The Gartner Hype Cycle for Emerging Technologies, 2017 focuses on three emerging technology mega-trends: 1) artificial intelligence (AI) everywhere; 2) transparently immersive experiences; 3) digital platforms. Walker elaborates:

> Organizations will continue to be faced with rapidly accelerating technology innovation that will profoundly impact the way they deal with their workforces, customers and partners. Our 2017 Hype Cycle reveals three distinct technology trends that profoundly create new experiences with unrivalled intelligence, and offer platforms that propel organizations to connect with new business ecosystems in order to become competitive over the next five to 10 years.

Figure 1.2 Hype Cycle for Emerging Technologies, 2018

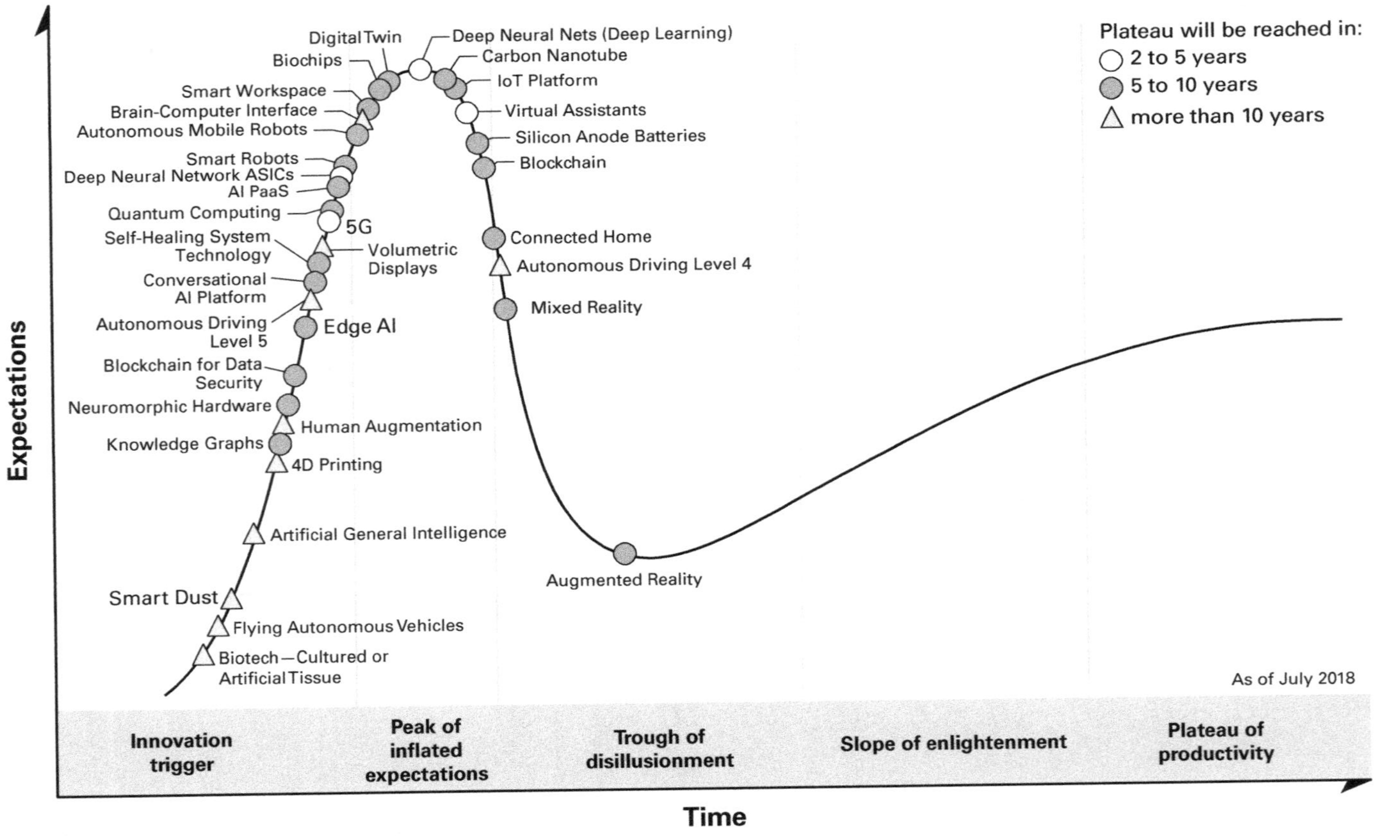

Expectations
Digital Twin
Biochips
Smart Workspace
Brain-Computer Interface
Autonomous Mobile Robots
Smart Robots
Deep Neural Network ASICs
AI PaaS
Quantum Computing
5G
Self-Healing System Technology
Volumetric Displays
Conversational AI Platform
Autonomous Driving Level 5
Edge AI
Blockchain for Data Security
Neuromorphic Hardware
Human Augmentation
Knowledge Graphs
4D Printing
Artificial General Intelligence
Smart Dust
Flying Autonomous Vehicles
Biotech—Cultured or Artificial Tissue
Deep Neural Nets (Deep Learning)
Carbon Nanotube
IoT Platform
Virtual Assistants
Silicon Anode Batteries
Blockchain
Connected Home
Autonomous Driving Level 4
Mixed Reality
Augmented Reality
Plateau will be reached in:
2 to 5 years
5 to 10 years
more than 10 years
As of July 2018
Innovation trigger
Peak of inflated expectations
Trough of disillusionment
Slope of enlightenment
Plateau of productivity
Time

SOURCE Adapted from Gartner (August 2018) © 2018 Gartner, Inc and/or its affiliates. All rights reserved. gartner.com/SmarterWithGartner

Some of the Gartner classifications:

Mavericks – companies willing to disrupt entire marketplaces eg Apple, Netflix, Uber, Alibaba, Amazon.

Leading organizations – fast followers of the mavericks; these might include P&G and other brands we know and trust.

Mainstream organizations – in a typical hype cycle this category decides to wait two to five years for technology to take a hold before it acts.

Conservative or highly risk adverse – this category could include government organizations that are, through no fault of their own, constrained. Or organizations that operate in a highly traditional sector, or a company that is simply very risk averse.

The power of innovative ideas versus capital

Walker discusses the accessibility of tech innovations, referring to a metaphorical 'class system' of businesses based on capital. He also discusses how in recent years, in order to succeed, the golden ticket has fundamentally become the innovative idea, and capital no longer stands in its way:

When considering their approach to embracing innovation, we have traditionally seen a pyramid where, at the base of the triangle is the major inhibitor, capital. This typically relates to money to take the idea to market, or to get a patent. The second major hurdle was connections, your network, being able to get in front of the right people – getting access to people and a distribution channel. The third and least important barrier to entry 5–10 years ago was the idea, the knowledge. Now the triangle has flipped completely. Now the barrier to entry is the idea. Financials don't matter nearly as much, and neither does the eco-system.

Flattening the companies through this lens provides us with a different perspective. For example, one division of a leading company could operate in this maverick way. In the leading category, AI is permeating all sectors. No industry is immune. With mainstream organizations, Gartner believes that we are seeing a utility-based use of AI. For example in financial services companies, AI is used amongst brokers or for the help desk function. This is a low risk footprint where the banks are taking advantage of natural language processing and chatbots for customer services.

Be careful not to get drawn into the misconception that success with AI and other tech innovations is only applicable to global organizations with deep pockets. Sometimes, the larger the business and the deeper the pockets, the more conservative they are in their mindset and innovation culture. Look no further than the automotive industry, which has seen Google and Tesla appear from nowhere and significantly challenge the major industry players with their autonomous and electric vehicles. They are bending the regulations and laws around how cars are manufactured and how they are sold to end customers. These companies came out of nowhere and were players. The same applies to Amazon in retail and Alibaba in hospitality.

Exciting chaos

For our next interview, we turn to another academic and one who specializes in marketing. Dr Elvira Bolat is a Senior Lecturer in Marketing, and Global Engagement Lead at Bournemouth University. She explains:

> The impact of AI on marketing over the next 2 years will be two-fold. Firstly, its 'buzz' impact will create this what I call 'exciting chaos'. Perhaps, AI will be the shortest word of the year in the Oxford diction- ary. It will be talked about by everyone, but also feared by all, even those who are knowledgeable. Why? Because, people think it is a disruption, which is larger than Robotics. AI is seen to integrate much deeper with a human's ability to think and this scares everyone. People will continue talking about cost–benefit, transformation of the work- place and industries, implications on privacy and independence of decision-making. However, the second impact will be unseen. Behind the scenes (we are seeing it now), industries are taking forward the ideas of B2B2C by creating plans to build business ecosystems where AI will be a critical resource to enable all parties to co-create value. In the next two years, we will not talk about AI anymore but our role in

the deployment of AI; what capabilities and competences are needed to strategically integrate and utilize AI. Giving up, by outsourcing the job of thinking to technology.

I believe manual and quite monotonous activities will be part of AI's remit. This excites me as I think this will drive the focus on creativity, which is very much a missing element. This will lead to operational productivity and strategic opportunities. It is important for everyone to see it as a bright future. Otherwise, we will create barriers to AI deployment and stop its progress.

Changing the face of PR

To really understand how applicable AI in marketing could be to companies across many sectors, we need to turn to the coalface, to a practitioner in the PR industry, who is advising clients daily on such related issues. David Gallagher is President, Growth & Development, International, at Omnicom Public Relations Group. He comments:

Setting aside the question of whether PR is still fundamentally linked to the news business, there are profound AI-driven newsroom technologies that are already changing the way 'the news' is created and distributed. If you believe media relations is still a big part of the PR consultancy proposition, and I do, we'll need to fully understand how our pitches, releases, statements and images fit within these new systems.

Media monitoring and reporting are already changing, and while these may be seen as 'low value' services they're not an insignificant revenue stream for many agencies. Media relations will also evolve quickly to accommodate new newsroom technologies to alter everything from breaking news development, product reviews and comment sourcing. And of course, influencer management – identification, engagement and impact analysis – is ripe for AI solutions.

There must be hundreds if not thousands of tools on the market, but one that has caught my interest is from Guardian Mobile Innovation Lab and a product they're testing called 'Smarticle' – where stories are broken [down] into core components, or blocks. These include basic details, a little context, embedded video and social media, and from there each return visit generates new, more detailed content based on signals sent by the reader, like how long they spent on the first block, or the time elapsed, or areas of initial interest. This has the power to obliterate the press release as we know it – and maybe create a whole new area of PR advisory services.

AI: the clever child

Clearly AI has huge power and potential, but the simple truth is, it is still in its infancy. AI is like a clever child, according to Peter McBurney, Professor of Computer Science, Department of Informatics, King's College London:

AI is good in some respects, especially in applications where there is lots of data of the right sort where you can apply these methods, but it is still fairly limited. This is the 5th big revolution in AI and every time they say we've cracked it but each time they haven't. It's currently focused around machine learning. Before that it was statistical classification, before that in the 70s and 80s it was expert systems; before that in the 50s and 60s it was called search, such as early programs to play chess.

What AI can't do right now, and probably won't be able to do for 30–50 years, is AI can't assess intentions. AI can't tell if you are sincere; this is an area where adult humans have an edge. We all learn to assess statements and decide if people are telling the truth or not. Of course we can be wrong but we have a much better judgement of it than machines. The methods used in machine learning and deep learning are observational and syntactical, so it would be looking at people's behaviours and listening to their statement and reasoning across all of that data, without going into their heads. That is a criticism of machine learning methods, that they are just looking on the surface and not the deeper meaning.

Renouncing problem solving

This book will not only announce AI in all its glory but will also explore why we should approach AI with caution and why businesses must not run before they can walk. Trevor Hardy, who is Chief Executive Officer at The Future Laboratory, has some very clear advice to offer CMOs:

> A lot of people are experimenting with AI, which is good, but without considering the consequences. Technology first replaced the need for muscle or strength, freeing many workers from heavy lifting. Now, machine learning and AI are allowing many to abdicate thinking just because machines can do it faster or better. There are many businesses that are racing to implement AI, but very few are considering the longer-term social, psychological consequences, or the civil liberties we may be giving up, by outsourcing the job of thinking to technology.
>
> It's changing the problem solving and thinking patterns of children who are very familiar with and in some cases dependent on AI to help navigate the world. Generations that are growing up with computing power as a thinking partner are instinctively co-dependent. The smarter and more useful AI becomes, the more analysis, thinking and decision-making we will hand over to it; as we look at this behaviour over years we are bound to see dramatic changes in people's ability to problem-solve and collaborate with others.
>
> Critical business thinking involved interrogating a problem, conceiving and considering scenarios to overcome it, evaluating options for action and then implementing a solution. But if you can go straight to a diagnosis without any thinking whatsoever, it changes the course of business and the cleverness and innovativeness of business decisions.

Privacy and personification

We have now reached a tipping point, one which has been building for over five years. The business landscape is being reshaped, driven by consumer pressure for transparency in the wake of privacy and fake news scandals such as Facebook and Cambridge Analytica. As consumers we have been perhaps naively unaware of the degree to which our own behaviours and activities have been recorded, sold and used to market to them. But now, brands are losing the little control they had left; power has been ebbing away since the late 2000s, given the proliferation of social channels that have allowed consumers to engage directly. Above all, people are reluctant to give their data away, even more so in a GDPR age where our right to withhold our data is recognized more than ever. To try and overcome this, Google has experimented with a value exchange concept of paying for data in order to keep showing ads.

The biggest win for marketers will be to exploit AI's potential for personification. Personification is an evolution of personalization, which marketers have been focused on for a few years. Personalization is the process of giving your customer the right message, on the right platform, using the right channel, at the right time. The main difference is that with personification you achieve this without access to their personal information. The next crucial piece of the puzzle is to give the customer a valuable experience, via the website or a chatbot for example. By doing so, the brand maximizes its chances that they will take action, for example downloading an app or signing up for a newsletter. We hear more about that from TGI Friday's in Chapter 5.

Fear and paranoia

Throughout this book we seek the invaluable insights from a lead analyst at Gartner in the US, as well as from experts at KPMG and PwC in countries ranging from the UK to Saudi Arabia. All confirm that AI is firmly in the paranoia phase, as the Hype Cycle illustrates. This is fuelled weekly, sometimes daily, by headlines, at least in the UK and the US, regarding job losses and robot warfare. These reports are not limited to tabloid newspaper but are often the work of highly credible sources. For example, according to a June 2017 report from researchers from the University of Oxford and Yale University, experts believe that AI will be better than humans at all tasks within 45 years. Their aim was to find out how long it would be before machines became better than humans at all tasks. The findings indicate that AI will outperform humans in many activities in the near future, including translating languages (by 2024), writing high-school essays (by 2026), driving a truck (by 2027), working in retail (by 2031), writing a bestselling book (by 2049) and working as a surgeon (by 2053) (Grace et al, 2018). It is therefore unsurprising that there are significant differences in openness and trust towards AI between the UK and China. As our survey, conducted using an AI market research tool reveals, fewer than 6 per cent of respondents from China reported that they would feel 'very uncomfortable' having robots in the workplace, compared to 25 per cent of UK respondents. Our case studies indicate however that few, if any, jobs will be automated entirely in the short to medium term. Rather, certain activities are more likely to be automated in a similar way to the manner in which the bank teller's job was redefined with the advent of ATMs.

The big questions

Trust, fairness and ethics are some of the major topics we tackle in some depth in this book. It is essential that governments across the globe work collaboratively with the private sector, as well as with the educators, the disruptors and the policy makers to ensure that we harness the potential of AI while mitigating the negative effects. A good example of this can be found in the UK where, in June 2018, the UK government announced an industry and government collaboration to develop the next generation of AI experts in the UK. Julian David, CEO of techUK, explains:

> This is more evidence of the Government's commitment to keep the UK at the forefront of innovation in AI. In building a world-leading framework for digital and data governance, the UK can be a pioneer in the development of responsible AI. We are pleased to see the Centre for Data Ethics and Innovation start to take shape. The Centre has a crucial role to play in creating the right environment for industry, academia, civil society, regulators and policy makers to consider how best to ensure ethical decision making is at the core of all implementations of AI. techUK also welcomes the investment and commitment made by industry and Government in the new industrial master's programme. Building the next generation of UK AI talent is vital to securing the UK's AI future.

Looking to the future

A glance at Gartner's Hype Cycle in Figure 1.2 reminds us also that AI cannot be contained. It will evolve rapidly, and there is a world beyond AI. Thierry Botter, Head of Airbus Blue Sky, comments on one emerging area of technical innovation that is closely aligned to AI, namely quantum computing:

> It's a very interesting time for quantum computing, with more and more transitioning out of the lab and into industry. We are realistic about the fact that there is still quite a bit of work that needs to be done, but nonetheless we believe in the importance of partaking in this work and positioning ourselves early on as a company that has an understanding of the technology, so that we can optimally prepare ourselves for the future.
>
> It's very hard to put milestones on the ground, but there is certainly a growing number of industries that are getting involved in quantum computing. Examples include the financial sector, the energy sector as well as the transportation industry. More and more people are thinking about this new form of computing and how it could be applied in their field. The start point for us at Airbus is to consider very pragmatic problems where we can anticipate an added benefit of this technology. There are certainly additional side benefits. I think it is very exciting and reassuring for our customers when they see Airbus demonstrating its commitment to being a leader in high performance computing solutions of all forms.
>
> My team at Blue Sky is the long-term research end of Airbus. Our research does not exist in a complete vacuum; it is obviously tied to internal business needs, which are the main drivers. We want to make sure that we address those needs, that we identify future needs and are able to answer them as quickly as possible. In time, teams would start to collaborate, for example those who are closer to the products and solutions. But we believe it's very important to offer a channel or a path for technologies to come in; this long-term view is essential even if it does mean that we are a little bit ahead of the times. With ever faster, more capable and more autonomous computational systems coming online, I believe it's essential to bring together engineers, scientists, business people, policy makers and educators to debate many of the

major topics with regards to ethics, the environment, frameworks, funding and policies. It's important to have conversations not just at a single company level but really to have it across different societal spheres.

Practical takeaways checklist: top 10 tips

1 We have only reached the tip of the iceberg with AI so there is no single bag of tricks available to the marketing professional.

2 There are hundreds of AI-related marketing tools available today. How applicable they are will depend on two things: a) how good they actually are vs how hyped they have been; and b) what the problem is that you are looking to solve.

3 AI is and will continue to be transformative in marketing. There are no brakes, so now is the time to research and begin to create a suitable strategy in response.

4 AI has unprecedented power to improve the human lot. It is a big responsibility and one that the marketing team will play a pivotal role in executing.

5 Despite AI's current power, it still requires logical reasoning, so we cannot outsource entire marketing problems to AI.

6 We will fall behind our rivals if we do not begin to apply AI to our marketing.

7 Today's barrier to entry with AI is the innovative idea, not money.

8 To ensure AI success in marketing, we need to first structure our data before we can begin to derive insights.

9 Marketers are the guardians of reputation and trust. We need to play an important role in considering the longer-term, psychological consequences of AI, such as the impact on our civil liberties.

10 Despite the hype, AI will probably not displace salespeople. The increase in qualified leads that an AI tool can create is creating a need for more people on the sales team to follow up on the qualified leads.

References

Econsultancy [accessed 9 July 2018] Marketing in the Dark: Dark Data [Online] https://econsultancy.com/reports/marketing-in-the-dark-dark-data

Grace, K, Salvatier, J, Dafoe, A, Zhang, B and Evans, O [accessed 9 July 2018] When Will AI Exceed Human Performance? Evidence from AI Experts, 03/05, Arxiv.org [Online] https://arxiv.org/abs/1705.08807

Ha, T-H [accessed 8 July 2018] Bill Gates Says These Are the Two Books We Should All Read to Understand AI. Quartz, 03/06 [Online] https://qz.com/698334/bill-gates-says-these-are-the-two-books-we-should-all-read-to-understand-ai/

Lavoie, J and Riese, J [accessed 23 July 2018] Leaders: It's OK to Not Know Everything. McKinsey [Online] www.mckinsey.com/business-functions/organization/our-insights/the-organization-blog/leaders-its-ok-to-not-know-everything

Oxfordreference.com [accessed 8 July 2018] Artificial Intelligence. Oxford Reference [Online] www.oxfordreference.com/view/10.1093/oi/authority.20110803095426960

PwC [accessed 17 July 2018a] AI Will Create as Many Jobs as It Displaces by Boosting Economic Growth, 17/07 [Online] www.pwc.co.uk/press-room/press-releases/AI-will-create-as-many-jobs-as-it-displaces-by-boosting-economic-growth.html

Tegmark, M (2017) *Life 3.0: Being human in the age of artificial intelligence*, Penguin UK, Harmondsworth, UK

The Japan Times [accessed 23 July 2018] In Breakthrough, Japanese Researchers Use AI to Identify Early Stage Stomach Cancer with High Accuracy, *The Japan Times* [Online] www.japantimes.co.jp/news/2018/07/22/national/science-health/japanese-researchers-use-ai-identify-early-stage-stomach-cancer-high-accuracy/#.W1XfvBJKgkh

YesICannes [accessed 17 July 2018] McKinsey at Cannes Lions: AI Doubles Revenue Growth, 04/07 [Online] http://yesicannes.com/mckinsey-cannes-lions-ai-doubles-revenue-growth-46568

The personalization paradox

Global appetite for AI and the changing customer journey

In this chapter, we take a deep dive into the changing customer journey, focusing our lens on the retail sector. We consider the role that AI is playing in this complex, interwoven web of marketing, sales and customer service. We also introduce the reader to a number of AI tools currently available to assist the marketing professional.

Put aside semantics for a moment; the term AI is actually a misnomer. AI enables the marketing team to provide a personalized experience to a user without being too intrusive. AI is already allowing the marketer to optimize websites, personalizing them for different users; for example, serving them tailored messages and designs that resonate, based on their profile and needs. The technology behemoths including Adobe, Verizon, Microsoft, Google and Facebook are driving this trend, one that will prove very lucrative.

The PR and communications industry is quickly changing, making it harder for PR leaders to make an impact using traditional approaches. With content marketing trends and innovative social media tools on the rise, PR experts should expect to see some major shifts over the coming few years. AI and other technological advancements, like virtual and augmented reality, mean that the pace of change will increase dramatically, bringing exciting new opportunities and challenges.

Marketing and advertising have been quick to adopt AI into their practices, but we've only touched the tip of a massive iceberg. As AI technology develops, reaching individuals at scale will be possible. Embracing the fact that AI solutions will be taking on the repetitive tasks like coverage reports, distributing releases and creating media lists, AI will allow savvy PR pros to actively focus on creativity and strategy – skills that machines simply cannot replicate (yet!).

The push and pull of marketing

Professor Michael Luck, Dean of Faculty, Natural and Mathematical Sciences, King's College London commented:

There have been for many years different kinds of AI techniques that have been able to do useful things for all kinds of business. This is the case both at the back end, for example managing files and data and organizing things, understanding how large organizations can be more efficient in general. But it is also about learning how to deal with customers and targeting things more accurately. To some degree they have been more or less simple. What has changed is the power and the data for this particular class of techniques. So that has changed the push. Deep learning has really made a difference to how people see the relevance of the technology. That is being pushed to some degree by the technology, and I think the technology will be relevant for some problems but not all problems. So there needs to be both.

In any organization, you need to understand what are the kinds of problems that will be suited to the different kinds of AI technique. You will be looking for a particular kind of problem to be solved. Not everyone will have those problems. The media are telling us we all need to have an 'AI first strategy' but not necessarily only learning of the areas that have had the media headlines. We need to look more broadly and decide where we apply those techniques and where we apply the things that have had less visible attention. Some areas of technology are being pushed forward because there have been exciting successes such as Alpha Go and the video game playing AIs. There is much more than that though. We do need to pull more now from the business side and try to understand what the problems we have are and which AI techniques will be helpful for those.

The changing customer journey

Paul Clarke, Chief Technology Officer, Ocado, stated:

Ocado is the largest pure play online grocery retailer in the world.
We do it like nobody else does with huge automated warehouses.
We build in-house almost all the technology that powers our end-to-
end e-commerce, fulfilment and logistics platform. As CTO, I have a
division, Ocado Technology, with 1,300 engineers, which will be closer
to 2,000 by the end of the year. Our technology estate is very broad and
deep spanning areas such as e-commerce, forecasting, routing systems,
robotics, AI, simulation and the real-time control of huge automated
warehouses.

We run on the intersection of IoT, big data, cloud, robotics and AI.
How we approach innovation is the alchemy that makes the magic
happen with those technologies. Of those, AI is the 'one to rule them
all'. It lets you do the really exciting things with the other technologies;
AI a recursive technology so you can use one generation to train the
next; it's the smart glue between services and systems, which is why it is
such an important component of Industry 4.0; it also lets you unearth
information, which has been hidden due to complexity or human bias.
It's in a transformational league of its own.

At the front end it is all about predictive analytics; what we call
building a broadband of grocery where we get closer and closer to
predicting and delivering the groceries our customers want without
them even having to order them in the first place. This is about how
we look at your previous orders and predict with time series analysis
what we think you'd like in your basket right now. But also, how we
personalize the shopping experience not only in terms of what people
like buying but also their different shopping styles and agendas. For
example, is it a top up shop, their monthly shop or do they just want to
buy something for this evening; are they a new customer or have they
shopped with us a hundred times before. It's very much about taking
the friction out of the process by using AI and ML.

AI is crucial to personalization, but there are lots of other frontiers.
Another one is voice, which AI has a big role to play in. Last year we
launched the first third-party transactional skill for grocery shopping on

Amazon's Alexa. This is part of a much bigger conversational interface journey. These are conversations which won't just happen on voice hubs in your kitchen but will take place in your connected car, in smart appliances, in chatbots, voice enabled mobile apps and call centres. These need to be one joined up conversation. Suppose I order some mangoes using Alexa in the kitchen and then I get in the car and decide I want a different variety of mango. Now I may be talking to a different assistant in the car such as Google Assistant or Microsoft's Cortana. When I refer to the mangoes, the assistant needs to understand it is the same ones I ordered five minutes ago. In other words, we don't want disjointed conversations. Ocado is building that back-end conversational engine to connect it all up. We have the context of the customer to do that. If you say 'add milk' to my basket, we sell 100 different varieties of milk, so to have a good idea of which of those you most likely mean, it's all about personalized learning. It's no longer appropriate to take a one-size fits all approach. Ordering from a 50,000+ item catalogue is very different to just asking Alexa to play one song. End points use technologies like Google Assistant and Alexa, Siri and Cortana, but the back end smarts that understand the context of our business and the context of the customer data, those are being built in-house.

That is a common pattern across what we do, because for some aspects of AI you need people with PhDs to roll own solutions, and for others you can use cloud-based services that are highly accessible, and you stitch them together to produce a solution. We do both. We use cloud partners like Google and AWS, and we also have our own experts in convolutional neural nets, natural language processing and reinforcement learning, and the rest of the basket of technologies that are in the AI umbrella.

Then there is the supply chain and forecasting what customers will want across each of our 50,000 products. That changes all the time as a result of weather, promotions, social media, seasonality or a celebrity chef recipe creating demand for a particular ingredient eg a vanilla pod. It's a moving target. Then you've got the control of these huge automated warehouses with huge opportunities for machine learning. In the new generation of warehouses, we orchestrate the swarming of thousands of robots in real time using an advanced machine learning based air traffic control system.

However, we also need to look after the health of the swarm itself. Does a particular robot need its batteries servicing; has something happened to its acceleration or deceleration. You can't do that with people watching screens. It wouldn't be scalable especially as we are now building these automated warehouses around the world for our Ocado Smart Platform customers; you've got to do it by sending all the data exhaust from the robots to the cloud and write a machine learning based healthcare system to look across the data from all the swarms and intervene.

At the last mile end of our business, you've got things like optimizing the thousands of delivery routes we drive each day. We do a lot with simulation, for example creating digital twins to simulate environments before they exist and even generating data to train machine learning before the real data exists. For example, building a complete simulation of a warehouse before we start to lay the concrete.

We're not like a normal retailer. We are this strange amalgam of being a retailer, a technology business and now a platform business as well. We have a mindset internally and a culture that is much more like a Google than it is a high street retailer. We are a disruptor in our sector. That process of self-disruption is key to what we do. We never rest on our laurels; however good a solution is, how can we make it dramatically better? We have multiple different kinds of research streams including a 10X division who are off placing bets that the main business wouldn't place but which if they come off, would be game changing for us. It's core to who we are; culturally we are quite unusual, quirky, risk embracing and unconventional. We take big bets in terms of the kind of solutions that we are building. You have to do that as a disruptor.

One of the key challenges the UK faces in responding to the opportunities related to AI is the skills deficit. Data Science and AI lie at the most overheated end of the software engineering skills spectrum and, as was noted in the above AI review, there is a massive shortage of graduates and postgraduates emerging with these skills.

What is not talked about enough is the fact that these skills lie at the end of a digital literacy pipeline that stretches all the way back to primary school. There is a massive amount more that government, NGOs and business could do to help manage the flow along the entire length of this pipeline and to plug the leaks.

But true digital literacy is much more than just teaching children to code. For example, we also need to teach them to be data literate. To understand how to organize and manipulate data, to gain insights from them, to visualize them, to build models from them, to understand the dangers of bias and so on. We also need to help our children understand the amazing possibilities and current limitations of technologies such as AI and robotics, the important ethical and philosophical questions around their applications, what it means to be human and so on. We need to find ways to maintain the level of interest in STEM subjects demonstrated by girls of primary school age which currently decays as they progress through the educational system. We need to be weaving this digital literacy throughout the curriculum.

However, this pipeline must not stop at college or university. It needs to continue on into the workplace, and here we need to do much more to incentivize organizations to invest in continual learning, particularly when it comes to subjects such as AI. We need to fuzz the boundary between education and work life. The existing linear system of 'go to school, go to college, get a job, do not repeat' is now broken. We need to prepare children for the process of continual learning and the inevitable reskilling that awaits them; we need to teach 'self-reinvention' as a meta skill and reframe the 'mid-life crisis' into an art form. But we need to do more, much more.

Many of the skills and techniques we are currently teaching our children will be as devalued in the years to come as the encyclopaedia has been by the advent of the world wide web. Instead we need to focus on teaching enduring meta skills such as collaboration, creative thinking, problem solving, intersectional thinking, mind mapping, goal setting and entrepreneurship.

If education is all about preparing the next generation for their future life and instilling a love of learning, then I believe we are failing in terms of the structure and curriculum of our current educational system. The current relentless focus on exams, tests and the regurgitation of mark schemes is consuming all the educational oxygen, leaving teachers with little or no time for spontaneity, for sharing their love of a subject and for just pursuing the curiosity of their students to see where it might lead. If we allow education to switch our students off the joy of learning, then we will do them an incalculable disservice.

So, I believe we need to completely rethink our education system from the ground up and, in so doing, future proof the underlying curriculum. We are currently tinkering at the margins. This is going to be a long-term game that we need to start playing now, because it will take 20+ years to work its way through the educational pipeline. That's why I believe we need to follow in the footsteps of countries such as Finland and remove the educational football from the political playing field because this is a game that needs to be played in a radically different way. Now is the time for political thinking and leadership that are truly holistic, agile, bold and disruptive.

AI will come faster than people expect and, like a tsunami, when it comes, it will just keep on coming. AI is like a new kind of drug many consumers have yet to get addicted to. But when they do, they are going to demand it everywhere. They will expect all their services to be smart and to play nicely and smartly with one another. We're currently at the stage of people being slightly intrigued when an app on their phone works out where they work and reminds them when it's time to go home.

Ultimately, we want to build a general AI that understands our business model, that understands our data taxonomies and has oversight of our end-to-end platforms. An AI that can answer questions about the business, that can help us work more efficiently and make less mistakes, that can act like the third gyro on an aircraft spotting the onset of problems that are about to impact us, that can help coordinate our suppliers, that can help our customers shop faster, with less friction and greater delight and so on.

Obviously that sort of general AI is beyond the current state of the art. So, we are focusing on building individual pieces of that puzzle that we will join up over time as the AI technologies and computing power advance. For us the current outcomes are less important. What's much more important are the learnings and competencies we acquire along what is now firmly for us, an 'AI and Robotics' first journey

Looking to the future of AI, an ideological war is waging between the optimists (such as myself) and dystopian in terms of predicting how our AI-powered future will play out. Listening to this debate one could be seduced into thinking we have a choice about whether or not to embrace technologies such as AI and robotics – we don't!

The UK may be an island but we cannot afford to behave as such. The technological tide is coming in all around the world, and playing King Canute will not end well. What we do have a choice about is how to make the best of the opportunities in front of us and successfully navigate the inevitable transformational challenges along the way.

We also need to strike the right balance between legislation and innovation. If we get this balance wrong and unduly throttle our innovation, then countries who prioritize innovation will have the advantage. Legislating against a future some may fear could lead to unintended consequences that are even more unpalatable.

CASE STUDY   Subha Ganesh, Global Head of Customer Acquisition at Reiss

In a digital world, you're often thinking more as a transaction rather than as actually an experience. But our aim is to bring the experience of the shop to the online world. Technology solutions like AI give the customer the feeling of having an adviser saying, for example, these are the shoes and bag that will go with that dress. We call that a bundle. It gives them advice on how to style up, with information on what other people have bought. In essence, it gives the customer confidence. They feel like they are getting a style guide or advice from the brand that is supposed to be an expert in that field.

It's early days with AI at the moment. To start, we had a few fears. The first was that personalization might be scary for the customer; we don't want to cross the line. We needed to know how much is good enough. Just as in a store you don't walk behind the customer; you give them space. Online, you also need to be there for them to call out to you. The second fear we have as a retailer is whether the data is actually available to make the correct AI integration. The machine can learn so much more if it has good data. This is the reason we work with a third party such as Increasingly, to get data quicker and cleaner.

AI will definitely impact marketing in the world of fashion retail. Firstly, it will help the retailer to give the customer what they want. Secondly, it will enable the retailer to identify the correct customer at the right time. This will enable marketers to make decisions and take calculated risks. AI will reduce guesswork and give the CMO confidence that their strategy is correct. Similarly, in merchandising, AI allows the retailer to buy what the customer is looking for and to stock at optimum levels. There will be less analysis of the past and more focus on future predictions.

Sri Sharma, CEO and CO Founder, Increasingly, said:

> AI will be increasingly used to both scale marketing, for example, AI content writing, and optimize marketing, for example, AI email copy optimization. On-site we will see more sophistication in how retailers engage with their customers on a one-to-one basis. In general, AI will solve all tasks that cost too much to scale manually and, secondly, AI will help us predict the future better. Automation Insights is helping companies automate content creation. Increasingly AI is helping companies cross sell with massive impact. AI in marketing has already happened; for example, Google Adwords is using AI in its core algorithms. Many innovations are on the cusp and proven. We are going to see mass market adoption.
>
> Companies need to recognize that if they don't innovate, their competitors will. To avoid getting left behind they have to test innovative solutions. This tends to be easier done by leveraging third-party solutions, as this feeds into the approach of succeed big or fail fast.
>
> Ethics can be a concern in the world of marketing; it's the reason we have GDPR. Using Google Assist to make calls pretending to be a human is also questionable from an ethics standpoint. As AI solutions get more sophisticated, we need guidelines from government to avoid trust breakdown.

AI is a general-purpose technology that touches all businesses and every part of all businesses. But, the reality is that it is a long and laborious task to see something happen in the real world. Speed of deployment is key. You need to deliver real-life instances as soon as possible, rather than talk strategy continuously. Companies like Kortical in the UK are offering a safe and fast route to embed AI in business.

Businesses that are much more proactive in adopting AI are seeing much greater returns, even at this early stage. McKinsey's 2016 report confirms this, concluding that those investing strongly in AI are already making on average 10 per cent more than companies partially investing or not investing in AI. Marketing Director Martin Harrison explains that Kortical's mission is to make AI available to all types of businesses. They believe it will be as ubiquitous as Excel and that it will have the same impact in a much shorter period of time. You would never have dreamed 40 years ago that Excel would be used across almost every business.

Their platform, The Kore, makes it easy for businesses to become AI enabled and to therefore grow faster and become more efficient. It enables Kortical to create bespoke solutions for businesses by automating a lot of the data science process. At the moment, there simply isn't the level of expertise available, so companies like theirs are having to do a fair amount of hand holding. Medium to long term, their ambition is to be a 'software as a service provider'. Harrison explains the three main things AI currently does:

1 **Prediction** – every business decision is a view of what the future looks like and what the future holds. The more data driven it can be, the more effective they are. AI and machine learning provide another boost; another layer to that ability to predict. Kortical recently worked on a project with the UK National Health Service (NHS), focused on predicting how long a recipient might have to wait for a compatible organ. The NHS had spent a few years refining this process, but using Kortical's model, they were able to improve it by 10 per cent in just over four intense weeks.

2 **Automation** – every business achieves efficiency by having repetitive tasks streamlined and standardized as much as possible. AI vastly increases the amount and depth of tasks that can be automated. It brings a layer of cognitive ability to decisions you are making; a layer that hasn't been there before. As a result, huge efficiency gains can be driven. Kortical recently worked with a UK high street bank, automating an email process. Historically, a small business would write to their bank and wait two days for a response. Emails coming into their business centre, which is a £1.4m cost centre, were assigned to the right customer service team. Before that someone had to manually open and read each one to figure out the appropriate ticket to raise. Using robotic process automation and AI, Kortical was able to automate this process in just over one month.

3 Innovation – is where things start to get really exciting. As co-founder Andy Gray explains: 'No business can stand still, particularly in today's world. The really interesting and exciting aspects of AI are where it's used to unlock new business models, new market strategies, new propositions'.

Kortical has also developed a chatbot called Obi, which does not require vast amounts of training data to get up and running. It can sit alongside a call centre operative and watch how they interact with customers. It learns and in a short period of time, it starts to replicate. A bank would therefore select two or three of its best call centre staff to train it. Within less than two weeks, it can start to add major value. Incrementally, it takes over and grows its own functionality. For most call centres, a relatively modest 10 per cent rate of automation can result in over £1 million in savings.

The market for AI at the moment is very immature. Businesses are still trying to figure out what their vision for AI actually is. They are also still trying to understand where their data is and how it can be structured for AI. At the same time, they are grappling with a severe lack of talent. The need is not only for data scientists but also the engineers who can manage the software development to deploy it. There is then a further requirement for project managers who can run an AI project; there is a real shortage in these areas too.

Harrison explains:

> At the moment, call lines are over-saturated. People prefer to chat but it's very expense for companies to always offer this. By improving the cost effectiveness of chat, the customer gets answers immediately. They can multi-task as they chat and wait for the answer. So it's a happy position – you improve customer experience and cut costs.
>
> Cost saving is definitely what is selling AI to businesses right now; it's what unlocks the budget. But we are definitely seeing improved customer outcomes and service, especially in chatbot and call centre space. And it's not, as some predict, a way to fire staff. Many are using it as a means of scaling more effectively because their teams can achieve more.

Loyalty marketing is one area where Kortical believes that AI and machine learning can make a huge difference. Next best action product recommendations are the holy grail of customer relationship management (CRM). One example of this in practice is a project with a large French grocery chain. This is a brand with 2.4 million customers and a terabyte of data. Using The Kore, they were able to offer time-dependent product recommendations, driving on and offline coupon redemptions. This six-week proof of concept project took into account which products would appeal, seasonal effects etc and resulted in higher conversion rates both on and offline.

One of the current challenges facing CMOs is that they are inundated with requests from different suppliers for multiple different point AI solutions. If a CTO or CMO is buying 5 to 20 solutions, all driven by the same set of algorithms, they are building up a huge amount of technical debt that isn't sustainable in the long term.

Kortical is working on a number of AI-related marketing projects in the targeting space. Sectors include insurance and financial services, where financial distress plays a key role. The marketer needs to make key decisions such as how to message users so they will engage; what is the optimal time and channel; which service will help them with their problem; and which imagery would be best. The Kore then creates bespoke machine learning solutions to build seemingly human-like intuition. It layers lots of simpler models in order to achieve a level of personalization. It can feel complicated, but it's actually not.

It's still early days and some may see these benefits as creepy. But AI is improving all the time, and as we adjust to it, the more it will just feel good and not jump out at you. Harrison concludes:

> Having a single customer view is beyond the wit of most humans. In our digitally enabled world, a human marketer simply can't manage or conceptualize across all of those touch points. By comparison, for AI, properly deployed on the right data, it is a relatively trivial problem. The technology is there. Now the key is unlocking the ability to deploy it. For years we've been learning to work with and be more like machines. AI allows humans to be more human.

AI marketing map 2018

Here are some of the AI tools now available to help an integrated sales and marketing team to automate time-consuming elements of the sales process. Clearly there are the major vendors, so we turn first to Bill Patterson, SVP and GM, Service Cloud, Salesforce. He explains: 'Artificial intelligence alone will not drive your business forward. AI must be connected to CRM data and guided processes so companies can create seamless experiences that put customers at the center'. Salesforce has combined AI with its CRM platform, further leveraging machine learning to improve the user's ability to engage and interact with customers in newer ways. Figure 2.1 shows a screengrab of Service Cloud Einstein.

In Chapter 6 we will hear from other major vendors such as Amazon Web Services (AWS). But it's also important to feature some of the smaller players who are disrupting the marketing landscape with their innovative tools, so we have listed a few of them here. The fact is, it's almost impossible to keep up to speed with the new tools entering the market so we've also included a handy guide, known as the AI Marketing Map 2018, courtesy of Overdri>e Interactive (Figure 2.2).

Base CRM

Base is an AI platform that learns from interactions that clients have with your sales team. The AI-powered Apollo program proactively provides feedback and intelligent alerts to your sales and marketing team, helping them to achieve their business development goals.

LeadCrunch

LeadCrunch uses an AI platform to filter good leads from bad ones.

Conversica

Conversica's AI-powered sales assistant qualifies leads but also engages them in human-like conversation, paving the way for the sales and marketing team to begin the customer journey.

Figure 2.1 Marketing Cloud Einstein

Figure 2.2 Overdrive Interactive: Artificial Intelligence Marketing Map, 2018

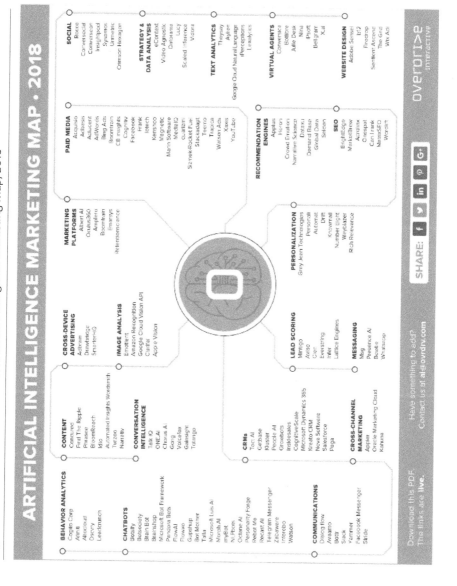

ARTIFICIAL INTELLIGENCE MARKETING MAP · 2018

BEHAVIOR ANALYTICS
Cogito Corp
Aprint
Altraccud
Darcy
Leadcrunch

CHATBOTS
Botsify
Botsociety
Brain Bot
Brainshop
Microsoft Bot Framework
Pandora Bots
FlowAI
Flexxo
Gupshup
Bot Mother
Talla
Microsoft Luis AI
Morph AI
myBot
N.i Photes
Octane AI
Personality Forge
Reibot Me
Recast AI
Telegram Messenger
Zabaware
Imperbo
Watson

COMMUNICATIONS
Dialog flow
Aveamo
Botr
Slack
Yammer
Facebook Messenger
Stride

CONTENT
Concured
Find The Ripple
Phrasee
BloomReach
Idio
Automated Insights Wordsmith
Twezoo
Narrativ

CONVERSATION INTELLIGENCE
Talk IO
ONE AI
Chorus AI
Gong
VoiceFox
Gainsight
Tatango

CRMs
Tact AI
Getbase
Kluster
People AI
Growbots
Insidesales
CognitiveScale
Microsoft Dynamics 365
Kreato CRM
Nova Software
Salesforce
Pega

CROSS-CHANNEL MARKETING
Appler
Oracle Marketing Cloud
Kahuna

CROSS-DEVICE ADVERTISING
Adbrain
Drawbridge
Smarter-IQ

IMAGE ANALYSIS
Emotient
Amazon Rekognition
Google Cloud Vision API
Clarifai
Apple Vision

LEAD SCORING
Mintigo
Aviso
Cer
Everstring
Infer
Lattice Engines

MESSAGING
Msg
Presence AI
Boonle
Whatshop

MARKETING PLATFORMS
Albert AI
Onuinia360
Amplero
Boomtrain
Emarsys
Retentionrnc ance

PERSONALIZATION
Grey from Techmologies
Personali
Automat
Drift
Knowntail
Number Eight
Wayblazer
RJch Relevance

RECOMMENDATION ENGINES
Applsas
Heiron
Crowd Emotion
Narrative Science
Dataxu
Demand Base
Gintbal Data
Sailoon

SEO
BrightEdge
MarketBrew
Acrolinx
Chaspot
Can I rank
MarketSEO
Wordai?

PAID MEDIA
Acquisio
Adbran
AdLucent
AdWords
Bing Ads
Sproantrain
CB Insights
Cognitiv
Facebook
Frank
Ioistech
Kenshoo
Magnetic
Marin Software
MediliQ
qualizm
Siznek-Rocket Fuel
Stackadapt
Teerno
Trapica
Watson Ads
Xaxes
YouTube

SOCIAL
Rosco
Conversocial
Converseoan
Insightpod
Sysomos
Unmetric
Crimson Hexagon

STRATEGY & DATA ANALYSIS
eContent
Video Agnostic
Databane
Lucy
Scaled Inference
Vistora

TEXT ANALYTICS
Theysay
Aylen
Google Cloud Natural Language
inPerceptions
Lexalytics

VIRTUAL AGENTS
Coaversica
BoltBore
Julie Desk
Niina
IPsoft
Belligrant
Xual

WEBSITE DESIGN
Adobe Sensei
b12
Firedrop
Sentient Ascend
The Grid
Wtx Acd

overdrive interactive

SHARE: f ⚹ in ⓟ G+

Download this PDF.
The links are **live.**

Have something to add?
Contact us at al@ovrdrv.com

InsideSales.com

InsideSales is a platform that collects relevant information for the sales process and generates analytics. This is then used to fully prepare the sales team.

Clarifai

Clarifai identifies people and objects in videos for easier media indexing.

Sailthru

Sailthru learns about customers' interests and buying habits and generates a classification based on the information. It advises the user on how and when to craft the message for optimal performance.

Analysing the customer journey

Dr Catherine Havasi is the co-founder and Chief Strategic Officer of Luminoso. She explains:

> Marketing teams focused on the customer journey know that to remove friction points and improve the customer experience, they need to listen to their customers. But manually reading through all of their Voice of the Customer feedback isn't feasible. Initial attempts to automatically process that feedback with AI have been limited because natural language technologies required billions of examples and months of consulting before they could successfully learn customer lingo.
>
> Over the next few years, AI advancements will eliminate that gap. Machine learning techniques such as transfer learning are already decreasing the amount of time and data required to train models for natural language understanding. These systems start with a knowledge base of millions of facts, so that the models start off with an understanding of the world. By giving computers 'common sense',

these systems can outperform other, more naive systems that must pick up that worldly knowledge from scratch each time.

The result is that marketing teams can respond much faster to input coming in from customers, identify trouble spots in the customer journey and take steps to fix them. That translates into higher customer lifetime value, a stronger, more loyal customer base and decreased churn rates.

As Figure 2.3 illustrates, Luminoso's clients have had success applying common sense natural language technology to the unstructured data of customer feedback. They find hot topics, trends, score drivers and emerging issues faster and more accurately than they would have by scanning survey results or capturing a few sample journeys from start to finish.

Bots as a Service

Tania Peitzker is Chairwoman and Company Director of a French company called Bots as a Service (BaaS) SARL – formerly known as velmai Ltd in the UK. She comments:

AI is already well advanced in marketing practices, in particular by the US tech giants. Think of Google, Amazon, Facebook, eBay, IBM, Microsoft and Apple tracking you wherever you go through GPS location services. The purpose is understood to be for marketing relevant goods and services to you on a personalized basis.

We are seeing most demand for AI from countries in mainland Europe, in particular Germany, Italy, Switzerland and France. Also parts of Northern Europe like Scandinavia and Estonia, but also China, Japan, South Korea, India and parts of Asia. Also the stronger and bigger markets in Africa and the Middle East. We are seeing demand from the private sector for automating processes, improving FAQs' capacity through advanced NLP chatbots or Intelligent Virtual Assistants (IVAs), direct sales and marketing at Point of Sale in large scale retail, in particular AI enterprise solutions like Bots as a Service, which velmai is offering to our retailer clients as of 2018.

Figure 2.3 Luminoso: analytics movie sentiment

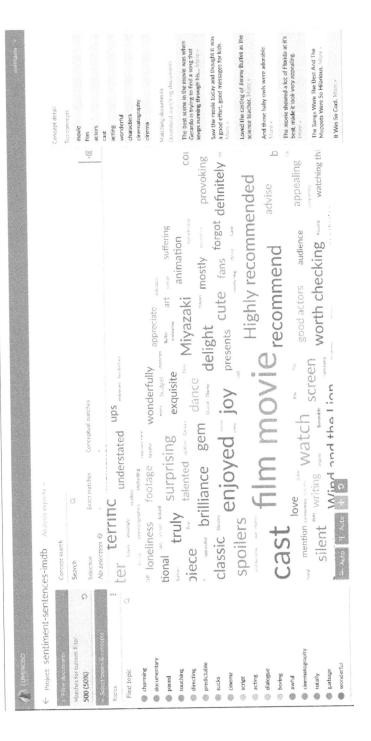

Our company, Bots as a Service SARL, is doing Greenfield Projects in heavy industry eg implanting our AI bot avatars in robots, augmented reality apps and holograms, in order to improve the productivity and acceptance of humans of these AI avatars as new forms of 'cobots'.

There is a lot of hype and misconception that thankfully the public is seeing through. Once they realize that they are already using AI (in smart cars, smartphones, online with browsing history, chatbots) and that AI is using them (with the search engines and bot spiders tracking our every move and desire for saleable future reference), then the public will see the AI ship has already sailed.

Personalization

Trevor Hardy, who is Chief Executive Officer at The Future Laboratory, explains:

One of the powerful abilities we've gained through AI is the personalization of marketing. People do not want personalized marketing; they want personalized products. There is a massive distinction between them. The creepiness of having marketing that knows you versus the products that are right for you is a fine line but an important one.

I have always believed that the best advertising is a better product. We have spent too much time applying the power of machine learning or AI to marketing a product or service rather than the product itself. Maybe that's the next step; the benefit is not the art of persuasion but more the art of design. In the last decade or so, we have become more robotic, as business and society increasingly value the abilities of machines: speed, power, efficiency. But rather than continue to mimic machines, AI will encourage people to put more emotion in decision-making and lateral thinking in problem-solving.

Machines in the last few years have developed much more ability for visual perception, speech recognition and decision-making; and in some cases doing these better than we can. It is now conceivable that machines will develop the ability to at least mimic or appreciate emotion. There are possible negatives, but the possibilities for business are exciting; allowing them to re-focus on human aspects of relationships, decision-making, customer service and experiences in contrast to the current focus on speed and convenience.

Finding correlations

We turn next to Peter McBurney, Professor of Computer Science, Department of Informatics, King's College London, who says:

In many applications, and marketing is a good example, we now have loads of data and we have these techniques from AI which we can use to figure out what is going on in the data and get patterns. These methods are allowing us to find loads of correlations and associations. There are far too many to act on all of them. So, the company has to prioritize. How is the CMO going to prioritize? They need a filter and a model, and that might be a formal marketing decision model or it might be that they have an implicit one in their heads. It should be really clear what that is so they can see what is going on. Knowledge of the domain is key to this success. There has been work on marketing models for 30 to 40 years. So, in a typical marketing model like this you would ask, who buys men's underwear? It's usually their partners. We can find that the same person who buys this underwear also buys lipstick, but it could be because it's women who are buying it, rather than men. People who are in the industry and in the market would know the answers to such a question. This detailed model and domain knowledge can help to filter out all of these false correlations. This then allows the marketing team to prioritize the decision-making instead of chasing wild hares.

In general, for a CMO, they should have a really good understanding of the customer journey. They need to really know that. There is a big danger, even without AI, that someone at the top of the marketing organization just gets so far away from customers that they lose sight of what is going on. AI makes that even more likely to be the case because you are putting in even more technologies between you and the customer.

Top management needs to remain fully aware of the customer journey. One success factor is for the CMO to get his or her hands dirty. They need to follow the example of McDonald's management who all spend time in store. Octus Telecom in Australia were the same, with managers spending a day per month in customer care. T Mobile's Chief Executive mandated the same.

What inroads will AI make on marketing?

One of the first areas will be in market planning, things like segmentation analysis. But AI will also make inroads in analysis of customer care and operations, for example the after-care aspects of marketing. These are the areas where you have lots of data. If it's an online company, then you will have data on which pages people have looked at before and after they bought. Where there is lots of data there is a natural place for AI.

All this fast processing will give the CMO a list of a hundred things that you could [use to] make a difference to the user experience. We simply can't implement a hundred things at once and even if we could it would be confusing for the user. So which ones are we going to pick? Which are the top five? So, you still need marketers with a lot of judgement.

Dominic Cushnan is AI Lead #AICommunity, Digital and Social Transformation at NHS Horizons. He states:

The opportunity of AI allows us to empower the person. Moving more to self-management of health and wellbeing. AI done right will allow nurses and other healthcare professionals to do the job they want to do, which fundamentally is to spend more time caring for the patient. With all the work being done around the omics, such as genomics, proteomics or metabolomics, AI will bring true personalization of care. The next 15 years as we cut through the fog of uncertainty we will see AI become more mainstream.

Practical takeaways checklist: top 10 tips

1   Personalization is a misnomer. Used properly, AI allows us to personalize without being intrusive.

2   It is now much harder to make an impact on PR and marketing if you retain a traditional approach and ignore AI.

3   It is crucial to understand the problems to be solved in order to ascertain which AI technique is best.

4   To succeed, you cannot rest on your laurels. Ongoing research and innovation will be key to maintaining a competitive edge.

5   We need to teach young people and our staff skills such as creative thinking, collaboration, mind mapping and goal setting.

6   AI is like a new marketing drug we have yet to become addicted to.

7   AI will reduce guesswork and provide the CMO with the confidence that they have the right strategy.

8   If you don't innovate, your competitors will.

9   AI is in truth still immature, and many companies are figuring out what their vision for it is.

10   Customers want personalized products not personalized marketing.

Transformational marketing and AI in tourism 03

A glimpse at the Asia Pacific region

In this chapter we focus our lens on the Asia Pacific region as well as homing in on the tourism industry, which has become one of the fastest growing industries in the world, with a global economic contribution of over US $7.6 trillion in 2016 alone (Statista, 2018).

With the tech revolution in full swing, there are a growing number of opportunities for travel companies to foster AI. Several leading travel companies including Expedia are already working with AI to improve and personalize the online customer experience, and it is likely at the forefront of how every reader is planning their travel today. In the past, it was necessary to visit or speak to a travel agent for the updates and information on trains, flights, hotels and last minute deals. However, this is no longer the case, as AI has created a much faster and seamless process for searching and planning your travel without having to leave the comfort of your home (or car or train).

To cater to the ever-growing market demand and the digitally adept customer – especially with the emerging Generations Z and U taking strides – travel companies are continually being forced to adapt to improve their services and better the customer travel experience. For instance, many travel and tourism sites use famous 'chatbots' – widely used mobile-friendly personal assistants that hone analytical and predictive capabilities alike to human travel agents.

As mobile booking is set to serve 70 per cent of all digital bookings by 2019, chatbots will become increasingly in demand in the travel industry, leading many to believe the traditional travel agent will begin to be phased out (Kutschera, 2018). As you converse with the chatbot, the machine learns and adapts, giving you the most appropriate information you need and learning from previous answers what you are looking for. The scope for chatbots is huge, as AI is helping machines outperform traditional search engines and real humans (including travel agents) in speed and efficiency.

AI is also helping customers by comparing and tracking hotel tariffs and flight fares over several suppliers to flag the best deals. These forecasting and comparison tools are ever popular with holiday goers, as they offer an efficient and cost-effective method for planning your travel online.

How AI is heightening customer experience in air travel

In addition, IBM have spotted ways in which AI can deliver personalized experiences and offer a competitive edge in travel solutions such as airlines, hotels and other travel services.

Airport technology is becoming increasingly advanced, from the airline customer experience to operational agility and maintenance. Most noticeably in recent years, AI in air travel is having the greatest impact in its ability to make things more personalized and more automated. New technology aims to create a frictionless and convenient experience from the beginning of the customer's journey, which usually starts at the airport.

For example, AI has already been developed and is operating in simple airport tasks in airports to enhance the customer experience. High-end airlines such as Qantas Airways are using self-service tech to reduce check-in times by over 90 per cent, while Air Canada created a self-service check-in system that is 80 per cent more cost effective compared to the traditional counter process. It is reported that almost 20 per cent of passengers now use self-service bag drop, and at passport control, 57 per cent of passengers would use biometrics instead of a passport or boarding pass across the journey, signifying a new era in airport experience (Skift, 2017).

Additionally, international hotel and resorts brand, Best Western, has recently turned to IBM Watson's AI to enhance the customer's booking experience. A recent report reveals:

IBM Watson Advertising and Best Western have teamed up to help take the sting out of summer travel with a new interactive AI-powered ad [Figure 3.1]. Best Western's Watson Ad personalizes vacation planning by providing consumers with travel tips and tricks, recommendations for local accommodations and special offers based on their travel preferences. Consumers can start a conversation with Best Western's AI-powered ad by simply engaging the ad and providing information on their current or upcoming travel plans. Through a series of dialogue prompts, the consumer will be guided seamlessly through a conversation about their travel needs, and the AI-powered ad will respond with tailored suggestions on how to make the most out of their vacation and how they can take advantage of Best Western's locations across North America.

Best Western's virtual 360° tour is a unique feature in the AI-powered ad that helps further personalize the hospitality experience. Through the tool, consumers will be able to virtually visit different Best Western properties that are available at their upcoming destination and get an immersive feel to better understand what each property offers. 'We're thrilled to partner with IBM Watson Advertising, as this cutting-edge AI-powered ad will allow us to drive more meaningful engagement with travellers, while showcasing all that today's Best Western has to offer', said Dorothy Dowling, Senior Vice President and Chief Marketing Officer for Best Western Hotels and Resorts. 'As the first hospitality brand to launch a Watson Ads campaign, we look forward to continuing our position as a frontrunner in innovation' (IBM, 2018).

Every city and country in the world will soon be looking to AI speaking on exciting innovations in the travel industry. Mark McVay, Chair of UKinbound says, 'Although the tourism industry is at its heart a people industry, AI offers exciting opportunities and any technology that helps to improve the visitor experience is of course hugely welcome'.

Figure 3.1   Best Western's Watson AI-powered ad

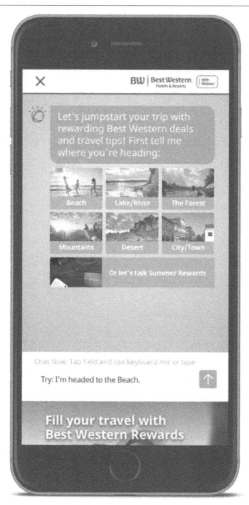

The future of AI in travel

As travel brands are witnessing first-hand the potential of AI applications in the industry, the potential impact of AI is finally being recognized. So how can AI be further honed in the travel and leisure industry?

Take a moment to consider how much time is spent daily on repetitive and administrative tasks in hospitality and retail, such as greeting customers, checking visitors in, filing their documents, photocopying their records. With advances in robotics and AI, many of these repetitive and time-consuming tasks can be done more efficiently using AI technology that's available today. This has opened up even more opportunities in the travel industry as hoteliers spot an opportunity to incorporate AI into their sector. This comes at a time when hotel chains are expected to continue their rapid expansion, as guest expectations are increasing and traveller needs become more diverse. It provides the opportunity for hotels to rethink costs and provide the differentiated customer experience guests (in the current digital age) crave.

Case study from tourism

CASE STUDY

Henn na Hotel, in Japan, is a robot hotel that has introduced advanced technology in order to provide guests with excitement and comfort. It boasts one of the world's first hotel robots to be equipped with AI. The multilingual dinosaur robot

Figure 3.2   Henn na Hotel, Tokyo

Figure 3.3   Robot fish, Henn na Hotel, Tokyo

Figure 3.4   TAPIA, Henn na Hotel's in-room concierge robot

at the front desk handles all of the check-in/check-out procedures. The hotel was the brainchild of Hideo Sawada, the founder of H.I.S., one of the largest travel companies in Japan. He explains:

> We use AI technology. The robots perform guest room concierge, reception work and on-site cleaning. The target market is young families. There was a little resistance from the elderly. But it is supplemented by human beings. The robots cannot take care of care, toddlers' care and unforeseen circumstances in our hotel.

The hotel promises to keep evolving according to changing times and needs. Sawada adds:

> I would like to develop full automated bed making someday…
>
> As the pictures illustrate [Figures 3.2 to 3.4], robots can be found across the hotel, even in the aquarium. Each guest room has its own concierge robot, TAPIA. It can recognize guest names and faces, available in Japanese, English and Chinese. TAPIA can also play games such as Rock-Paper-Scissors, as it can recognize the shape of hands. It can also turn on/off the room-light/air-conditioning/TV and delivers a fun and unique experience to our guests of all ages…
>
> AI will alter marketing in the tourism and hospitality sectors within the next 5 to 10 years. It requires initial cost but running costs can be reduced. The number of elderly visitors to Japan will increase. My estimate of the timeframe by which AI will become mainstream in this sector is around 10 years.

Japan and China forums

AI has already made its mark across a wide array of business sectors, and the hospitality industry is fast catching up with this trend, promising incredible innovations.

Colin Fox is Group Marketing Manager for English Lakes Hotels Resorts and Venues. He is also Chairman of Lake District Japan

Forum and Marketing Director of English Lake District China Forum. Fox comments:

AI in the hotel industry will be the most important factor in not only marketing but of course sales and service. Hospitality is the most important word in hotels, and we believe that human interaction with the guests at all the available touch points is how we deliver the best guest experience. At English Lakes we have a philosophy and culture that empowers our teams to really make a difference at any sensible opportunity. This +1 philosophy has created the foundation for our high level of returning guests, great review ratings and even a big contributor to staff retention. However, although I doubt that this personal interaction will ever diminish, the emergence of AI will become so prevalent to offering a quality service and experience. The Disney themed hotel in Tokyo with robot dinosaurs is not something I see happening at Low Wood Bay in the near or distant future. But AI will be important in providing the information to deliver a faster, more efficient check-in, better room set up on arrival, knowing what each guest really wants when they arrive and during their whole stay.

In a GDPR era of data collection and storage procedures and restrictions, it will be so important to have the right information and know how to access it and utilize it well (very well) to deliver the experience that will make guests happy that you have it and happy for you to keep it.

Although guest experience will play a massive part in the ability to retain information and the guest returning because of that experience, it will be also hugely important to use AI to create the bookings and get the new guests in the first place. Using SEO to create traffic to a website and providing great UX and bookability online is and has been the main focus at English Lakes for many years. It is how AI will become more the driver to getting that traffic, standing out from the crowd and generally being seen. Being booked. Google is number one now but will it be Alexa, Siri or of course people asking Google instead of typing long tail phrases to find what they want. Voice recognition is already important and will become key to gaining or at least not losing market share.

Two very important international markets to the English Lake District are China and Japan. The former having its very own social media platform and unique digital landscape that seem to be way ahead of what are commonly used in the west. AI will take the level of understanding and development to a new level and to position ourselves to compete with other countries and domestic competitors for that market we will have to adapt and provide, understand and react. In office visits around Japan, we have experienced lots of great examples of AI in action and probably experienced many more without even knowing. In an office in Tokyo whilst waiting to meet some of our top contacts at their very grand board room at almost the top of one of the very many skyscrapers in the city, I found myself interacting with a robot in reception. We were attending as the Lake District Japan Forum and it knew we were coming and knew more about us than expected. Although the few minutes of waiting was entertaining and novel, it was just a simple and effective use of making our very short time in reception memorable. Meeting humans was our objective and promoting our part of the world in their offices was and will stay a priority, but interaction and information retention is how we need to look into our future strategies and delivery of those strategies.

AI is here, and it's coming to a hotel near you soon

Simon Greenbury is Conference Director, Future Global Opportunities for UK Tourism Director Cheeky Monkey, an agency that is championing UK tourism. Greenbury explains:

One thing is for sure. AI in the travel industry is in its infancy, but there is no doubt the sector's development is the future. Applying AI tools will open up an abundance of opportunities – some we don't even know yet – that will improve all aspects of the traveller's experience. It will help simplify decisions, shorten the process of buying and deliver a more personalized service.

It is hotels in particular that are recognizing the importance and power of AI and video recognition to get better knowledge of their clients via personal data provided on reservation or previous visits.

It will not be unusual to have customers checked in via a mirror equipped with facial recognition; rooms adapted to needs and requirements of guests; mattresses with sensors to record movements of those sleeping which could prompt hotel staff – perhaps robots – to offer them a coffee when they wake up. Data will be able to determine what the clients' habits are to encourage them back by offering a tailor-made experience or sell additional products. And not forgetting AI driving the future of transport systems. Dubai are aiming to have 25 per cent of their system driverless or smart by 2030.

As the travel industry is powered by a vast magnitude of data, and since data is the horsepower for AI, it is no wonder that the combination of AI and the travel industry is promising powerful things. Lee Hayhurst is the Editor of Travolution, a UK-based travel technology website, magazine and events business. He explains:

> Much is being promised from AI in travel, and if only half of that is delivered it will be truly transformative. All travel firms are looking to operate more efficiently and to be more relevant and personal in the ways they deal with all customers on digital platforms; however, they must be wary of over-automating in such an emotive industry. The most likely immediate impact of AI will be felt behind the scenes where travel firms that manage and supply products like airlines, airports, hotels, tour operators and other intermediaries have incredibly complex systems handling the huge amounts of data that the sector generates.

Also speaking on the growing use of data in the travel industry is Samantha Mayling, Editor of Travel GBI. She comments:

> Judging by the increasing amount of coverage of artificial intelligence in the travel trade press, it seems the technology is being adopted by many in the industry – such as airlines, hotels and online travel agencies. It is helping to crunch vast amounts of data, to look at booking trends and customer needs, and help predict what consumers want. I think it will be helpful behind the scenes, with data analysis, and perhaps there will be more use of AI with chatbots, but I think the scenario of robots checking in guests at hotels will remain a gimmick for at least the next two or three years. More people are using voice (Siri, Alexa etc) so I think they will increasingly search for holidays

this way, but I doubt that many will book holidays via voice in the next couple of years. There will still be a role for expert travel agents who have specialist knowledge, but AI can certainly help consumers narrow down their choices. I like the idea of this Icelolly service, dubbed 'Uber for agents' which will connect consumers with high street agents if they're searching for something complex. This is an interesting quote too, suggesting there is still a need for the human touch for a while yet: *Icelolly, which generates 40 million search queries a year from about 20 million visitors, said holiday planning had 'become a little robotic'.*

Despite the enormous benefits that utilizing vast amounts of data in the travel industry can generate, it is vital that steps are taken to ensure we maintain consumer trust so that these advances can continue without resistance. Greg Clark, current UK Business Minister, comments:

> Let me give an example that might appeal to those of you who have flown on an economy airline. If you travelled with a family member bearing the same surname, did that airline's booking system automatically place you together? Or did it automatically place you in non-adjoining seats, to try to extract from you a premium payment for the 'privilege' of travelling together? On such questions will the trust of customers be won or lost. Once again, government's role is to bring forth an environment in which companies treat customers with the respect they deserve, not use data and digital technology to exploit them.

Resisting change

With such huge transformations sweeping industries, and as the new replaces the old, we must consider the challenges to seamless transition.

Debbie Marshall, Managing Director at Silver Travel Advisor comments: 'Older people tend to be change resistant and many would be horrified at the thought of dealing with a robot, which is how they view AI. A recent story on the news reported that the work of GPs may soon be done by AI and this is viewed with some disbelief by the older sector'.

This belief is echoed by Stan Jeffreys, an 80-year-old from London, who comments:

> The generation today who are in their 70s and 80s at times cannot take in all the new inventions and technology. There is talk about planes in the future without pilots, cars without drivers, and robots in the home doing the jobs we are used to doing ourselves. To us, it sounds like H.G. Wells science fiction. Most of us do not use the Internet as we do not have the means or the motivation; the same with Twitter and Wi-Fi.

Nonetheless, as Debbie Marshall suggests: 'There's a grudging acceptance that it's inevitable and might even be more effective'. But can the older generation in fact be thankful for this progress? Marshall comments:

> I really can't believe that robots will replace sympathetic and experienced travel consultants but can see how back office functions will benefit. I believe that developments such as hands-free check-in, and facial recognition instead of room keys, can really help older travellers, making a hotel stay a more relaxing experience. Fumbling through pockets and bags searching for reading glasses and keys can be stressful!
>
> I am old enough to remember life before the Internet and remember how some companies resisted websites initially, dismissing them as a fad, before racing to catch up once they realized they were here to stay. Ditto mobile friendly websites and more recently social media. Ignore new technology at your peril – many older people have the time and desire to get to grips with the digital world and are now the fastest growth sector on Facebook!
>
> Looking at the future, and the role of AI, companies need to be proactive and understand how it can best work for their business. Employ people who are ahead of the game and don't be Luddite about it or bury your head in the sand. The same goes for blockchain, which is clearly another new innovation and disrupter which is here to stay.

Hunger for AI in Asia Pacific

As we focus in this chapter on the Asia Pacific Region, we turn now to Reboot.AI, a Hong Kong based machine learning and AI solutions provider, co-founded by Dhruv Sahi and Matt O'Connor. Clearly in this region, China is the big player in AI and is a country that is taking it very seriously. In July 2017 China laid out a development plan to become the world leader in AI by 2030, aiming to surpass the United States and other rivals technologically and build a domestic industry worth almost US $150 billion. Released by the State Council, the policy confirms that the world's second-largest economy intends to invest heavily to ensure it is at the forefront in the technology, which many industry observers believe will one day form the basis of computing.

However, China is moving in a direction that some people might view as dystopian. What for many was a far-fetched concept in the Netflix series *Black Mirror* depicting a dystopian future, seems to be becoming a reality. Recently, Chinese authorities decided to trial a new social credit system that has uncanny parallelism to the *Black Mirror* episode 'Nosedive'. In this episode, society is judged based on their interactions with other people. Better interactions lead to higher numeric ratings as well as more opportunities for the individual, and vice versa with poor interactions. Similarly, in China, citizens will be 'scored' between 350 and 950 based on their impact in society. Good deeds such as undertaking charity work and donating blood boost their score, while cancelling a reservation or befriending someone 'undesirable' will lower their score. Higher ratings will unlock rewards within society, from shorter hospital waits to cheaper public transport, while lower ranked citizens will have slower internet speeds and restricted access to restaurants and hotels.

For businesses in Asia that are outside of China, there is a lot of fear and a sense of not wanting to be left behind. Sahi explains:

> There are two kinds of people interested in AI, and it is quite easy to tell the difference. On the one hand, there are those who actually take it seriously; they know about AI and are really invested in it. They have a serious business problem or point of pain and they want a solution. On the other hand, there are the players for whom AI is about the PR buzzword and the marketing. They simply want an AI solution to boost their name.

There are a number of areas of low hanging fruit. One is workflow automation, which is far less flashy and less impressive in comparison to some of the more consumer-facing solutions. Another area is the back office, where you find in insurance for example, natural language processing for processing claims better and faster. These tools will compound the competitive advantage for a company. Companies want a solution that is just plug and play, that fixes everything. But we're not yet at that point.

For many companies the driver for AI is efficiency in general. It is an element of cost saving. It's about spending less on human labour, spending less time on external resources and spending less just on waste in general. If I automate a process, I don't have to pay external consultants and humans as much. So companies need to start by looking at the things that are hurdles in their everyday work.

From a marketing perspective, if you have a great recommendation system, it appears to the end customer that you can almost peer inside their mind and know what they are thinking; that you know what they want to buy before they buy it. That is the kind of competitive advantage that comes from having the data. Good data and good algorithms can create cost cutting and increased value to the end consumer. It's a tight rope of the push and pull of convenience and Big Brotherhood. The April 2018 Facebook and Cambridge Analytica scandal is a prime example of this. A lot of Facebook's features are great and people like the convenience. It's really easy to connect with people; it's easy to get suggested friends; to see friends' recommendations and places. Having this data about us makes our lives more convenient. People want these features, so companies build them. But on the flip side, people are sometimes unwilling or unknowingly giving away more information than they realize.

Data's magical powers

Let's turn the clock back to what marketing was 10 years ago. We put advertising out. People saw it and those who wanted to used to call us. With AI it is getting to a point where you can target the kind of people you/the AI think will be a good fit for your product. It's about understanding the customer better; understanding your products and what you are selling better. You can now create more complex relationships and find similarities where before you didn't see any. You can start bundling products together, for example understanding buying patterns better like a classic Walmart diapers and beer. The data informs you that customers tend to choose this. You get tiers and tiers of understanding which allows you to segment the customer better. It's like they have magical powers.

Navigating the landscape

Reboot.AI's focus at the moment is on helping people to understand and navigate the landscape. There is a huge desire to implement technology, and there is a lot of technical expertise out there especially in China. But there is a big disconnect with regards to real business problems. They want to use AI to solve these problems. They know AI is well suited, but they don't know how to go about it.

Sahi and his team are helping clients to understand for example that this is something image recognition could help with or natural language processing. These are algorithms that can achieve that. He continues:

The smarter companies are not reinventing the wheel. They are using the models that Google has trained on and are then deploying that model in a targeted way. So they use open source python or open source machine learning AI implementations and connect to more powerful models. So a lot of what we do is helping people to build that second layer on top of models.

Standing on the shoulders of giants

Sahi concludes:

If we zoom back 10 years, if you wanted to be a web developer you really needed to get a computer science degree. You needed to know the technicalities of optimizing an algorithm. Today, the barriers have been drastically reduced. Many people can become a web developer by standing on the shoulders of giants. That's because there are so many packages out there that you can implement. You can still build what you need without necessarily knowing all the details of how it works. This same trend is beginning to and will play out with machine learning and AI. You only need the PhD if you are trying to invent a new algorithm or trying to redefine the forefront of the field; the 'how' it works. You don't need to go that route if you want to implement it and build it. The talent is out there in full stack developers. People think it's so much more complicated than it really is.

Marketing disruption

Travel industry marketing is changing as a result of these advances, and operators need to adapt. Here we take a closer look at current trends and what they mean for marketing, not only in the travel industry but also across all sectors.

We spoke to Gerardo Salandra, the CEO at Rocketbots, and the Chairman at the Artificial Intelligence Society of Hong Kong. Salandra is a self-trained data scientist who trained in Python. Today he works as a consultant in Hong Kong, advising clients such as McDonald's and the Hong Kong Jockey Club. He advises them on how to use AI for marketing, advertising and in-bound lead generation:

> Marketing is the next space to see real disruption from AI. Just look at the giants like Salesforce with its marketing cloud. They have changed their entire strategy from being about marketing automation to being AI first. Their Einstein engine is integrated into paths created for customers, enabling trend analysis and pattern recognition. In 24 months, I believe we will see big disruption.

According to Salandra, the likely impact on marketing will be in a number of key areas, notably:

1 **Inbound marketing** – Content is getting smarter. You can now see how people react to certain content, which is allowing AI to offer mass personalization. This means that you build content for a particular customer segment. Even the content itself can now be generated by computer. This applies in Europe and the USA but not in Hong Kong.

2 **Advertising** – is another area. Using neural networks, you can now
   create an advertising network which personalizes content for the user.
   The advertising then follows you with retargeting, but it won't show
   you the same ad again. It keeps adapting; it isn't prefixed. The machine
   will alter different colours, different backgrounds and different lines
   of text. You never have to tell it what to try and when. This is used
   to do AB testing. The same recipient will get the ad and decipher
   whether they react better to green or blue, for example. Next time, you
   can apply that knowledge, even if it's for another client, because the
   machine is learning over time. It gets to the point when the advertiser
   may know more about you than you know about yourself.

Salandra continues:

> Metisa is a start-up in Hong Kong which offers mass personalization.
> Such technologies and solutions are available today. But the reality is
> that most companies are still struggling to move to a digital world.
> Many have the budget for AI but still haven't survived the digitization
> wave. How can they use AI for selling when they don't even have CRM
> in place? Jumping these steps leads to massive failure. Many Fortune
> 500 are trying to skip these steps.

Retooling in a technological world

Despite the advent of consensual acceptance for AI, the sector continues to speed forwards, creating fantastic opportunities and machines
that can undoubtedly be harnessed for personal use, or by businesses
across several industries, for their benefit. Jon Young, Research
Director at BDRC Continental, comments:

> The development of AI will make it easier for consumers to get what
> they want, shortcutting current processes. For example, we currently
> search for something by typing into Google, clicking and then scrolling.
> But if, for example, we have AI alternatives to finding what we want
> (ie Alexa) then the Google process will become archaic and redundant –
> our children will look at it in the same ways that we currently look at
> the Yellow Pages! I (personally) am already thinking that typing is a
> laborious process! We'll simply ask what we want without needing to

type, click and scroll. This has huge implications for digital advertising, much of which is facilitated by the Google search. The same is likely to happen to YouTube advertising – who needs YouTube when Alexa will play whatever you want? TV advertising? Well what place for that, in a world where all your programmes will be pre-recorded! Perhaps the focus will turn to 'live events' that can't be recorded eg sport?

I've no doubt that the 'Alexa process' will be monetized for marketing, but if (say) in the AI arms race, the USP becomes lack of marketing disruption (unlikely as every single technological shift seems to be accompanied by marketing), then we may see marketing companies scrabbling around for alternatives. Traditional means of marketing – such as posters and brochures – are unlikely to be affected by these changes. People will still physically move around, and the arresting presence of a large billboard or a beautiful brochure will still have an impact – and with digital options reducing may become more important. We've already seen this with holiday companies.

The plethora of digital messages makes the physical more powerful, as does the evolutionary desire for people to physically own something (in a world where everything sits in the cloud). As such we've seen physical holiday brochures return, in much the same way as we've seen the physical book return in popularity. This shouldn't be a surprise – we are conditioned to believe that physical ownership represents success and resources – key to our survival.

Practical takeaways checklist: top 10 tips

1 Ensure you are using AI to solve real business problems.

2 Don't jump on the AI bandwagon for fear of being left behind. Have a clear strategy.

3 Don't reinvent the wheel. Research the open source tools available to you and 'stand on the shoulders of giants'.

4 You can't jump steps. Many companies have a budget for AI but have yet to survive the digitization wave.

5 AI will be prevalent in tourism for offering quality service and experience.

6 Many older people are resisting change but beginning to grudgingly accept it.

7 AI is making major inroads in hospitality and retail, such as greeting customers, checking visitors in, filing their documents, photocopying their records. Many repetitive and time-consuming tasks are being completed more efficiently using AI technology.

8 Data will be able to determine what the clients' habits are to encourage them back by offering a tailor-made experience.

9 Despite seeing the advantages, people are sometimes unwilling to give away too much personal information.

10 Many believe that marketing is the next space to see real disruption from AI.

References

IBM [accessed 23 July 2018] Best Western® Hotels and Resorts and IBM Watson Advertising Introduce AI-powered Ad to Help Consumers Personalize Vacation Planning, CISION PR Newswire, 29/06 [Online] www.prnewswire.com/news-releases/best-western-hotels–resorts-and-ibm-watson-advertising-introduce-ai-powered-ad-to-help-consumers-personalize-vacation-planning-300674484.html

Kutschera, S [accessed 9 July 2018] Travel Statistics to Know About in 2018 and 2019. Trekksoft.com, 04/07 [Online] www.trekksoft.com/en/blog/65-travel-tourism-statistics-for-2019

Skift [accessed 9 July 2018] From Novelty to Game Changer: AI and The Future of Work in the Travel Industry, 20/09 [Online] https://skift.com/2017/09/20/from-novelty-to-game-changer-ai-and-the-future-of-work-in-the-travel-industry/

Statista [accessed 12 July 2018] Global Tourism Industry – Statistics & Facts [Online] www.statista.com/topics/962/global-tourism/

Swant, M [accessed 16 July 2018] Best Western is Turning to IBM Watson's AI to Help Travelers Plan Summer Vacations. Adweek, 29/06 [Online] www.adweek.com/brand-marketing/best-western-is-turning-to-ibm-watsons-ai-to-help-travelers-plan-summer-vacations/

Transformational 04 marketing and AI in Europe

Case studies from telecoms, banking and built environment

In this chapter we switch our focus to Europe and to three industry sectors that are making major inroads with AI, namely telecoms, banking and the built environment (comprising property/real estate, construction and facilities management).

We begin with a feature on Paul O'Brien, one of the directors of research at BT Labs at BT plc (BT), a British multinational telecommunications company. BT Labs is part of BT Technology, which manages the systems, networks and technology that support BT's customer-facing businesses such as EE and Openreach. Its *raison d'être* is to build and operate BT's technology infrastructure and future proof the company by anticipating new and emerging trends, maximizing benefits for both BT and its customers.

O'Brien joined BT 27 years ago and did so because of BT's work in AI at that time. Having studied AI at university, he was a researcher in natural language processing in an earlier generation of AI known as symbolic AI. Three impressive decades in AI means that BT – and O'Brien and his team – has experienced many generations of AI technology. Each time a new generation of AI comes around, BT applies it to the problems and challenges faced by a telco.

Many levels of distortion

O'Brien compares the current hype around AI to the one that accompanied big data:

> It distorts people's perception and understanding of what is possible and what it can do. We've gone from a situation where we might hide the fact that we're using AI applications, as was the case 10 to 15 years ago; then it simply wasn't a selling feature. Now, we're at a point where if we put an AI badge on anything, everyone wants it.
>
> Some people are swallowing a lot of hype and not just from the media but from vendors and researchers. There has been talk of Terminator scenarios, with cognitive capable machines replacing everyone and taking over the planet. This exaggerates the reality of where we are at. There has been a significant step change in AI pattern recognition capabilities, which is driving improvements in areas such as image, video and speech recognition. This is a far cry from sentient machines. A more sensible view is that there will be wider opportunities for augmented-AI systems, where we combine both human and machine strengths to assist in a task.

Instead of being drawn to the hype, businesses should be seeking to understand the realm of possibility and what the latest generation of AI means for their company, so they can embrace it and focus on those opportunities.

BT has deployed a lot of AI in its operations, for example enabling the 30,000 strong field engineering workforce out in their vans to improve customer service. AI algorithms are used to optimally structure the workforce, predict level of demand that's likely to come in, diagnose faults, schedule work allocations and support the field engineers when on a job.

An AI algorithm determines how they are structured; when to anticipate demand eg repair volumes, due to adverse weather conditions.

> If we can accurately forecast repair volumes, we can more accurately plan our capacity and better meet customer needs. This is possible as a result of modelling a vast amount of operational data including 30 years' worth of weather data. These tools use a range of AI technologies from smart optimization techniques, to chatbots and the latest

generation of deep-learning neural nets. These support our people to ensure they make the right decisions. This is just one strand of how we are deploying AI, but it is having a massive impact on our business.

Securing many column inches of press coverage over the past year or so, chatbots are a very public application of AI in marketing, made possible by speech analytics interfaces. But as O'Brien warns, this does not mean that the back-end systems will understand what is being said to them. Asking Amazon Alexa to switch on the television or provide a weather forecast is a narrowly defined request which AI can respond to. But if you are trying to have a more complex interaction such as work out why a customer's TV image is poor, you need a sophisticated back-end knowledge base to support those kind of interactions. In many cases companies do not have that knowledge accessible in their back-end systems because it is either embedded in people's brains or not captured sufficiently in their systems.

> People are selling AI based on the speech analytics piece, but this front-end bit only addresses a fraction of the overall challenge.
>
> Our view is that the main challenge is how to make your business AI ready. AI technologies are changing rapidly; businesses need to have a platform that enables them to rapidly exploit these technologies. This is much more important than having lots of point solutions.

Amazon and Facebook have been very effective at exploiting the marketing analytics opportunities of AI, because their entire infrastructure was geared around data analytics. Their architecture, their systems, their mindset; everything is centred around the value of data and what value you can extract from it. That is not always the case for lots of traditional businesses who may lack the infrastructure but will have valuable data assets. If you are an insurance company, you most likely have vast quantities of data. A start-up does not have that history and longevity of data. So, with reference to Gartner, they might be laggards in terms of their digital infrastructure, but they will not be laggards in terms of the depth of their knowledge. Fifty years of motor incident history is therefore a very valuable resource, which, from marketing, sales and customer service perspectives, needs to be exposed and leveraged to best effect. These traditional companies now need to become AI ready by digitizing their data and applying some smart analytics to extract insights.

One of BT's best applications of AI is in cyber security. Its role is to detect anomalous behaviour like malware attacks. Smart AI algorithms learn what normal patterns of behaviour look like. If anything breaches that, it is flagged up as an anomaly to security experts in our security operations centres. In the old data analytics world, a company would have collated it all; run analytics over it and in a week or so would be able to detect strange behaviour. Using AI tools with the latest computer power, we can achieve this more or less instantaneously and have systems that adapt over time. This is allowing BT to protect customer networks, and the quicker you identify it, the quicker you can respond and protect your network.

> Technically, we've had a step change in AI capability. This is driven by the availability of large quantities of data and significant computer power, so we can now run multi-layered neural networks in a relatively short time. This technology will gradually pervade all different parts of the business, as with previous generations. However, its biggest impact will be in how it augments humans rather than replaces them.

Switching across to banking now, where we hear from Mark St John Qualter, who leads the AI capability in commercial and private banking at Royal Bank of Scotland (RBS). He has a strategic role to mobilize the capability and bring the right people together to deliver it:

> There have been a lot of false dawns in the past about AI. I recently visited India where I met a guy who did a PhD in AI 15 years ago. At the end of that he couldn't get a job; at that time people had hired a lot of staff and spent a lot of money on it and it just hadn't materialized. It was very unfashionable so he went and did something different. Since then he went on to start up his own company and now the tables have completely turned and he's in demand globally.
>
> There are three reasons why AI is here to stay this time: 1) the transactions from our digital age mean that we now have data of the scale and the format that we need, which we didn't have before; this is as a result of the way we live now; 2) we now have the architecture to host the data and the pipe – or broadband – to move data around; in the cloud we have integration into AI tools so you can mobilize and

move data around cheaply, and store and manipulate it; 3) we now have the computer processing power at the right economic cost.

This means there is less risk in doing AI now. There are basic formats like chatbots and voicebots that people are starting to use and deploy, and they are finding some really positive outcomes from it.

With regards to AI in marketing, segmentation is important. Traditionally it's always been a building block of marketing. Companies and banks in particular have been very bad at segmenting customers. They have typically segmented them around their own vertical organizational structures. Post-2008 we saw a focus on customer centricity, and banks have now realized that they have to change the way they operate. To date, segmentation has been very set in stone around commercial, personal and corporate customers. Now, AI allows the data and tools to create much more dynamic versions of segmentation, recognizing that customer needs are changing and that the value of those customers is changing. With AI you can almost anticipate what those needs are and create bespoke engagement. Banks and big organizations generally get criticized for 'not knowing us'. Data and these tools will now allow us to much better understand and analyse not only customer needs but anticipate the drivers going forward, which all feeds into how you market them.

One big question to address is what will human beings want to do. Their tastes will change as they get hold of new things. There will be a place for the high street as people do like to go shopping. The key to survival for those on the high street is for customers to see how you are different. It's around customer experience and innovation, engagement and understanding the *zeitgeist*.

Regulation and the law is a bit behind the run rate but they are aware of it and they are catching up. The emphasis is around good design by those who are designing the AI applications. It needs to be relevant and have utility; there has to be trust. In my lifetime AI won't replace humans. The best application is where it augments and enhances what humans can do. People need to feel that they can escalate to a human being.

At the moment there are lots of books on bias. When we build it we need to ensure that we don't build our own biases into that. AI is just a branch of technology. It's not synthetic human beings. Thirty years ago we got rid of open core trading floors and went into dealing rooms, then computer trading. It's the same. Think about markets. The press like the hype and sinister overtones.

The challenge for practitioners is to be very clear and accountable. It will start with markets eg banking or securities; work is underway. They will need to come up with frameworks as they are having to do with bitcoin and blockchain.

It's like dynamite; you use it to blow tunnels through mountains and create transport systems which are good for people. Or you can blow people up. Many things can be done wrong and can be destructive.

Humans are limited by our Darwinian pace of evolution. By comparison machines can train each other. There is a risk, but it's up to us to ensure that we control it and design it in such a way that you mitigate those risks.

One academic who believes that the banking sector is ripe for disruption is Danielle George, MBE, FIET, Professor of RF Engineering, Vice Dean Teaching and Learning, Faculty of Science and Engineering, The University of Manchester. She comments:

The British financial tech firm Revolute has applied for a European banking licence. Using AI, they want to break the dominance of the bigger banks. They are chipping away and winning. They have slick mobile apps, no fees, you can have an instant overview of all of your finances and not just the one bank that you are logged onto. They have just under a million users who consider it as their bank and their spending card.

With this in mind, we now turn to Dr Patrick Hunger, CEO of Saxo Bank (Switzerland) Ltd:

Technically speaking, a robot like Pepper does everything right. He communicates, he asks questions, he explains data protection. He even applies and executes banking regulations such as PSD2 for bank accounts. But it feels odd. This is all hard coded. It's not the embracing psychological safety we actually wish for in communication. The human reality is very different and we need to tap into that. This is what we aspire to do with Pepper. From a conceptual perspective, when we started in June 2017, we had to consider the environmental perception and the organizational change curve. We started out assuming that the outside world will be intrigued at the outset, but we just needed to ensure that Pepper was as intelligent as possible. From the organizational perspective, we projected that staff members in a digital bank such as Saxo Bank would be interested in working with a robot and would go through that change process positively relative to staff with traditional incumbents, possibly not diving too deep into rejecting the transformational process that we were in.

In the external space, with regards to our clients, what happened was that they were initially extremely fascinated by a humanoid robot that was entertaining. He wasn't able to do any sense-making ie conversational communication. But he smiled and was able to ask if people wanted to take a picture, which both clients and guests did. But the problem is, that the fact that his body shape is built to resemble the human body led psychologically to our guests wanting to socialize with him. But the challenge is, Pepper could not socialize because he is not able to deal with the unexpected in conversation. The fact that he did not deal with the unexpected created anxiety with our clients and they got bored and irritated and they walked away and lost interest. But we really wanted to get to the next stage, because we hooked Pepper up with IBM Watson. Pepper would have done beautifully in connecting the knowledge dots, but we never got to that because the socialization process was never completed.

The only guests that had that imaginative power were kids. When Pepper didn't work they didn't really care. They just took that as an invitation to create a world in which Pepper didn't do anything physically and verbally. But grown-ups had an expectation; they are in a bank and their expectation level is high and it just didn't resonate. When we put that into a contextual perspective, as soon as the description complexity, the knowledge complexity and the client complexity are all high, the outcome at least today is either human to human interaction that can be augmented, or religious – something transcendental. Pepper had only an existence in an isolated domain and with very precise and short questions. If a client or guest left that stage, it just became very unsatisfying for all of us. That taught us a lesson, and interestingly, people hardly ever asked the questions we expected or the ones we programmed into Pepper.

The questions people ask are extremely diverse. Which reminds us that we banks often think that we are client centric, but this example shows that clearly we are not really. What was more worrying is what happened internally from an organizational change perspective. We're always hearing talk about organizations needing to be agile, needing to work in teams and tribes, but there is only one single question that matters for your staff. We tried various approaches to experimental inclusion; we even tried to incentivize people knowing that this was from a behavioural perspective least appealing. We went out to sales staff and said 'create the dream journey with Pepper. Augment your pitch; make it more interesting. Use a humanoid robot and try to get into a different kind of discussion with your clients'. But they weren't able to do so. Possibly they lacked the imaginative power. The only question they really asked was, 'what's in it for me? Why should I do that?' At the outset we had a possibly wrong perception of how people are intrinsically motivated, how people are interested in creating a change process and how people are interested in tapping into a transitional space. It doesn't help when they read media headlines about slashing 10,000 staff and doing everything automated and being much better off and more efficient. The challenge is you don't have an answer for every individual in your organization. You can lead by example as much as you want and try to create a culture, but as long as you don't have that question/answer, you're going to have an uphill battle against loss aversion.

So the conclusion that we have was that there is no need for Pepper as a service. In the financial space where we go more into mobile devices and to tech that is less and less visible, it was probably not a client-centric idea to create an autonomous physical trading lounge in which Pepper would end up discussing financial realities with our clients. The bottom line is if a robot resembles a human body, psychologically something very different – that means human – happens. This is what needs to be taken into account, and defining and designing a reasonable context is crucial. We can definitely see such humanoid robots being used in hospitality, in railway stations, in hospitals and airports; depending on what it's supposed to be doing it may make sense from a recipient perspective.

It's also important to consider regional and cultural differences. In Japan, they are culturally open to robots, because of animism. They don't make a distinction between inanimate objects and humans. They allocate a spirit to subjects and objects, which is not common in Switzerland. Today, with the limitations it has, the humanoid robot operating in a bank and interacting with clients just doesn't yet work for sophisticated interactions. It's not about Pepper. One of the misconceptions I hear is that if you use enough technology, it's going to work. But technology is a commodity and there is a line of democratization. Change management capabilities to the contrary are scarce and linked to your staff and respective individual personality traits. They need to be able to work and deal with anxiety. Employees need to be able to understand and embrace the fact that there is no safety net, which puts loss aversion as a behavioural cornerstone of humans centre stage. So from a hiring perspective, this is what I try to do. Skill sets I can buy; leadership is my job; the change management angle is key. Still we're seeing too many traditional mindsets, and Pepper was for us a good example to test the waters and observe human behaviour. Change management is key. We failed fast and we continue to experiment and to expose our staff with uncertainty. If we get the mindset right, technology will follow the human purpose.

The transformational mindset

We now move our dial across to the built environment, a sector that comprises property, construction and facilities management. We begin by taking a deep dive into a case study of a very charismatic young Asian entrepreneur and business leader called Syed Ahmed, who has deployed IoT and AI technology and pioneered the world's first smart hand drying range for the corporate washroom sector. Syed was born in Bangladesh but came to London with his family at just nine months old. He was brought up in London's East End, where he lived with his industrious parents and five sisters who were born in the UK. Syed will be familiar to many of our UK readers, as he featured in the well-known BBC series *The Apprentice* in 2006, departing just before the finals. Because of his ethics and family focus, Syed is a local hero. He has supported his parents' ambitions and helped put two younger sisters through private education, but sadly lost one sister to illness four years ago.

Syed is passionate about the spectrum of entrepreneurship and how technology can change an industry. Today, he is co-founder and managing director of Savortex Ltd, a dynamic technology company that has teamed up with Intel and pioneered the world's first smart hand drying range, which digitally reports on real-time usage data and shows an advert in response to hands being dried (Figure 4.1). The company's vision is to transform wasteful and costly commercial washrooms into sustainable and profitable smart spaces. Syed founded the company in 2006 when he met inspiring product engineer Peter Williams, and after three years of research and development, building several prototypes and overcoming all the expected financial challenges – Savortex was born. In a very candid, passionate interview, Syed gave us some illuminating insights into his journey; one that has seen him exploit technical innovations to flip an industry on its head. The path to success has not been a simple one. It has required tremendous strength of character and resilience.

Figure 4.1 Savortex Intel Inside adDryer

In the early days, Syed was looking at how he could create a unique market position; one where he could differentiate his company from goliath brands such as Dyson and PHS. Back in 2011, there was energy efficiency in this industry but no innovation. One-third energy consumption just wasn't sufficient as a differentiator. The spark came when Syed read an article from global intelligence firm Frost and Sullivan. He soon got to know the Managing Director very well and embarked on his journey whereby Savortex would lead with innovation: 'If you want to lead an industry, you need a transformational strategy. You need to think in the unknown and outside of the box. Many leaders feel scared and vulnerable, fearful that they will fail or not understand. Look at where the masses are going and do the opposite'.

Syed believes that if you have complete transparency, you have the ability to demonstrate value and to open up a transformational business model. He decided to focus on transforming data collection and making it fun. There were multiple layers to this. First, he focused on the corporate sector where IoT could be deployed within commercial buildings. Second, he had to consider how to set new standards; how to use technology to drive more savings and create a new route to market. He soon realized that the answer was via landlords, asset managers and facilities management (FM) service providers. By creating a portal, he could demonstrate the washroom's consumption traffic, thereby adding real value.

The third part was the business model. One of the biggest challenges he faced was cost. His smart move was to devise a method of paying the asset back to the client in a shorter period of time. Monetizing the data and transforming the user experience provided a powerful way of scaling the business. The product was offered for free, and his company kept the advertising revenue.

One of the major challenges that Syed faced was involving the entire business. He was effectively asking the business to change how they manufactured, produced, sold and marketed the product. In the meantime, he was investing over £1.5 million, with no immediate signs of reward. Gradually, he involved different layers of the business, drawing them into his imagined future. Having painted the financials, he managed to secure the board's backing. PR and marketing supported it immediately, and then he took on all the departments, one by one: 'I had to be 300 per cent committed to the vision or die by it', he explains. 'It took three years to design, develop and launch it. Two years of challenges, learnings, failures and working through different suppliers'.

His management team invested £0.5 million pounds, and he began the process of raising £1.5 million. A two-year journey of trials, tests and pilots ensued. He failed and tried again. Conceptually it sounded great, but the reality was often very problematic. For example, putting the hand driers into a basement in Bermuda was a major obstacle because it was under concrete and there were issues with the IoT sensors and components communicating.

Simultaneously there was a business to run and revenue to bring in while they were developing a new strategy and product range. Two years in, Syed confides that he was in a very lonely place. He had re-mortgaged his home and raised the numbers. He knew the rewards were potentially huge, but he needed all of his conviction to get through this turbulent period.

Syed was pitching the concept to Managing Directors and CEOs of FM companies, but it was falling on deaf ears. He had hundreds of meetings, often with rude CEOs. 'This is not a technology for us!' they would claim, fearing change. They simply didn't want to collaborate. They were arrogant; this most likely stemmed from ignorance, which was blocking the opportunity for real innovation. They were fearful of new processes; fearful of the unknown; they didn't want to be the first. One notably said: 'I'll wait and go later!'

All of this reluctance was in spite of a compelling business case that showed how the technology would deliver up to 98 per cent on operational savings. It was also resource efficient as a result of the data, enabling businesses to achieve the same results with 50 people rather than 100 and provided a revenue share.

Syed cites the example of an office with a canteen where staff would typically leave the building to go to a nearby Costa. Using the ad dryer, corporates could offer a 10 per cent discount, enticing users to stay in the office and use the canteen.

Thankfully the penny finally dropped at a point where Syed was nearly bankrupt. 'I had purpose', he states. 'I was prepared to leave behind the legacy; to change a principle and make it a better industry.

I had to have an open mind or get left behind. I had to turn hidden risks into profitability'.

Syed is a great role model for the new wave of CEOs that today's changing business landscape requires. Namely, an executive, irrespective of age, who has clearly gone through a fundamental shift in their thinking. His message to entrepreneurs is simple but effective: 'ask yourself how you can innovate', he recommends. Think differently about routes to market and alternative ways to generate revenue; about the way you connect to the workforce. Is technology making your business sustainable? Is it driving efficiencies?

Syed certainly had vision, tuning in early to a technology that is now one of the major growth areas. According to Juniper Research (2018), there will be 50 billion IoT connections by 2050. 'Look at what the phone has done to communications', he concludes. 'The same phenomenon is happening with IoT and AI. But frustratingly, lots of press are deliberately spinning strange stories, driven by fear'.

Dr Brian Atkin is Director at The Facilities Society and Co-Founder of AI in FM. He comments:

> AI will automate most routine tasks in administration and an increasing proportion of managerial tasks. In marketing, it is likely to offer previously unconsidered options and alternative strategies based on the analysis of big data.
>
> The construction industry is not a homogeneous sector. There are the professions – architecture, engineering, surveying and project management – and the supply chain – construction companies, specialist contractors and suppliers – as well as clients of the industry. Architects' needs and interests are very different from supply chain firms.
>
> Those tasks that are already supported by software will be the first to be affected by AI. It is the next step. Design, planning, procurement and cost management are examples of where AI is likely to score early wins. AI will automate design detailing for architects and engineers and automate project planning and scheduling for project managers and construction companies. I believe it will take 8 to 10 years for change to embed in day-to-day practices in the construction industry. Healthcare, media services and security services are a few of the sectors which are starting to gear up now. In terms of action, the construction industry needs to talk more to software developers, and sooner rather than later.

Resisting change

One company with an established track record in the FM sector is FSI (FM Solutions) Limited. Peter Tyler, Director of Technology, comments:

> From a business point of view, I believe that AI type technologies will start to become trusted sources of information. This will be in the form of human assistance and will not result in job losses in the short term. The wider adoption of AI into business will come post two years, where some decision-making may become completely automated by machine learning algorithms.
>
> Areas where factual based decisions are made will be the first targets for AI, such as financial transactions and risk assessments. Workplace monitoring, both physical workplace and staff engagement will also see an uptake in AI techniques. This will drive automation and targeted services. The structure of organizations will start to change as companies adapt and move to digital business, and as such there will be a stronger reliance on technology skill sets such as data science.
>
> The FM sector is not gearing up well for change. The sector has some forward-thinking companies that are driving new innovative products and services; however, FM is primarily based on traditional business models and commercial frameworks which are inherently risk averse. In FM, there is an abundance of historic data held within CAFM and IWMS systems; tools that can utilize this historic data with machine learning techniques to create predictive models will be the driver to move away from planned maintenance. IoT, BMS and AI combined will address the smart workplace.
>
> Change has already started within the software industry supporting FM; however, FM providers must start building strategies for adopting digital FM within six months. In terms of a framework for success, companies need to build out a strategy that moves them into a Digital Business model. Experiment with technologies such as AI, IoT Platforms and High-Productivity Low-Code Platforms. The need to be agile in business from a services and IT delivery will become even more important to the success of the business. Organizations that do not accept the inevitable change will be at serious risk of becoming obsolete.

AI can be a touchy subject, and just because we can technically achieve something, it is not always good to do so. Any AI that uses personal data is especially sensitive for ethics, where using this data to categorize, track and manipulate people can be very emotive eg Facebook. I think the driver of AI is the promise of the wider benefits, where automation can be made smarter, decisions can be made without prejudice and lives can be made easier. From a business perspective, the driver is based on providing competitive advantage in services, leaner teams and general cost reduction. To achieve this there will need to be diversification in the toolsets and platforms, as if every company in the same industry used the same tools, they can expect to get similar results and therefore less competitive advantage. Skill sets within business will change, with growth in IT functions such as data science, BI and product delivery. To keep agile, investments in monolithic applications such as ERP will decline and investments in AI, IoT and high productivity development platforms will increase. It will be imperative to the business success to be able to adapt to market movements quickly, which is not possible with traditional IT and ERP systems.

Scott Newland, Treasurer and Secretary Executive Board, EuroFM, comments:

The Facilities Management sector is evolving and the future has some big changes in store. Whilst the industry is constantly striving to provide the best service to clients, a greater focus is now being placed on creating the ideal building, whether this is a school, hospital, workplace or public facility. Front of house is an essential service for businesses across the world as reception staff are tasked with creating a positive first impression as visitors arrive. Ensuring that front of house service delivery is as good as it can be is a top priority for facilities managers.

The conversation with clients, which focuses on improving the workplace, must continue, but we must also start stepping out of our comfort zones to discuss how best to embrace new technology to help businesses maximize productivity. With such a vast uptake of AI and robots predicted, organizations must plan for the integration of new technology. Rather than simply installing a device, it is essential that these actroids represent your company in the same way a human would. Policies are important in this respect, helping to maintain your brand values and brand perception. The type of actroid required will also vary depending on the sector in question. Technology companies, for example, are likely to want to be perceived as forward thinking and will therefore be drawn to actroids which show a large array of capabilities. On the other hand, a manufacturing plant may be more interested in actroids which can take on repetitive jobs to help increase productivity over long periods of time.

The benefits of actroids in the FM space are extensive; not only can they interact with visitors and carry out tasks, they can also work unsociable hours and can have a dual purpose – something a human cannot do. Evening shift robots can double up as security guards, monitoring the building and being the first line of defence should any security threats occur. This is especially beneficial in high-risk environments such as testing laboratories, which may be targeted by activists. With the development of the Internet of Things, this will also enable such robots to be linked to CCTV allowing the robot to analyse any security issues much faster than a human.

For the time being, the human touch and ability to interact with visitors is irreplaceable; however, organizations need to start preparing for a future filled with actroids, robots and AI as technology continues to develop rapidly.

Tom Lipinski, Founder of Ventive and Q-Bot, explains:

We design and build robots for specific construction tasks, like insulating or surveying buildings, getting into hard to reach places. For example, if an operator gets a robot into a particular unexplored space and it still needs to be controlled by the operator to get somewhere or achieve anything, the operator in turn needs to understand the following: where we are; what we are doing; why we are doing it. Then the device, for example an insulating robot, can insulate an area by itself, but then it needs to be navigated there by an operator. If we give robots full autonomy to explore and map new areas, they often head for the door and try to escape, because they just go on exploring. So, there are limits to AI and autonomy in the construction space just because the tasks that people are doing are quite varied and require ridiculous amounts of improvisation. The amount of computing power and decision-making and improvisation in the brains of even an average builder is actually immense. We can't possibly match that in a machine today. Instead we use them to augment and to supplement. It will probably be another 5 to 10 years before such machines can self-locate for example.

We are years away from a time when the machine will ask 'why we are doing this?' Whenever you set an AI up on a task, it will follow its core program or instructions. It is not just because the computing power isn't there. We may need to start writing software in a completely different way, which means going back 100 years and starting again, which, may or may not be possible. Robots, currently, are just glorified tools such as power drills or figures. We are nowhere near any sort of self-awareness or consciousness; for that we are talking 40 years or more.

There's a tendency in anybody's brain to concentrate on the hyperbole. But the reality is that in the past five years, we have made almost no progress. We have better sensors, better hardware, electronics have moved on a great deal, but we have made zero progress when it comes to developing artificial intelligence in this sector.

The problem is we still have absolutely no idea how our brains work, so we are in the dark. Consider the start-ups with their new amazing tech. Fifty per cent of the time, these claims do not even materialize even in a period of five years after spending billions on it.

Transformation in real estate

JLL's 2017 global report series, *Workplace: Powered by human experience*, reveals that experience is a primary differentiator whenever individuals engage with an organization and that it should play a core role in every company – both strategically and operationally. A place of work is more than a property. According to JLL, it is a living environment that helps individuals and businesses craft and experience a rewarding fusion of life and work.

Dr Marie Puybaraud is Global Head of Research at JLL Corporate Solutions. She explains:

Real estate has evolved to become a strategic lever for transformation, enabling organizations to achieve broader business agendas and ambitions. It is a two-way dialogue in a landscape constantly changing and evolving. The Future of Work is JLL's outlook on the changing world of work and its impact on the next generation of corporate real estate. It is articulated around five dimensions driving fundamental changes for corporate organizations: financial performance, operational excellence, human experience, digital drive and continuous innovation.

Dr Marie Puybaraud believes that governments could play a significant role in enabling AI to really take off:

> Firstly, in terms of creating awareness of what AI is in simple terms. Secondly, by creating working research groups to work on this new discipline and the different facets of this discipline. Thirdly, education is required; specialists in AI need to be trained today. It is very clear that our research on human experience is extremely relevant for the HR community, and the CRE community is taking this topic as an opportunity to work closer to HR.

There is significant investment in AI in the pipeline. According to Accenture (2017), 85 per cent of executives report they will invest extensively in AI-related technologies over the next three years. The workforce is changing – between 20 and 30 per cent of the working population is already working in the on-demand or gig economy (Raconteur, 2017).

Organizations are exploring new solutions around automation and robotics. In the period 2018–20, the expected annual growth rate of sales in service robots for professional use is expected to be between 20 and 25 per cent (Wadlow, 2017). How this will impact the morale of staff is not clear at this stage as the volume of AI companions is still far too low and invisible to employees. A lot of AI solutions work in the background with no interference with humans.

The findings of the report are based on consultations with decision-makers from 40 corporations around the world and the results of a separate, anonymous survey of more than 7,300 employees working for companies with more than 100 members of staff. The survey covered 12 countries, and the respondents were aged between 18 and 65 years. Countries where employees were surveyed were: Australia, China, France, Germany, India, Italy, Japan, the Netherlands, South Africa, Spain, the UK and the United States.

The JLL study reveals that organizations can benefit in measurable ways once they realize that the experience they create for their people dramatically affects their level of engagement, sense of empowerment and feelings of fulfilment at work. Key insights include:

- Nearly 70 per cent of participants agreed that happiness at work is the best ingredient to guarantee a unique work experience.

- While large corporations continue to attract more talent (61 per cent) than the smallest ones, almost half (46 per cent) of respondents said they aspire to work in a start-up environment and that they crave an entrepreneurial culture.

- Only 40 per cent of respondents revealed feeling very engaged at work on average and consider 'trust' and 'kindness' – which can be fostered through agile workspaces – the biggest positive impact on their engagement at work.

- Only 52 per cent of employees admitted being entirely satisfied with their current work environment. In addition, 42 per cent revealed feeling completely ready to move from their personal desk to open-plan offices or unallocated seats, in order to access new innovative workspaces.

- Almost half of respondents (47 per cent) think that being able to concentrate in the workplace is a top priority, calling for a stronger focus from companies on giving employees a choice about how, when and where they work.

Neil Murray, EMEA CEO of Corporate Solutions at JLL, said:

> In a world increasingly driven by data and digital innovation, the future of work is actually more about people than you might think. Organizations can no longer only focus on providing space to work, they need to create places that enable people to achieve their ambitions. Appealing to what people want can have transformational benefits to businesses.

Dr Marie Puybaraud adds:

> Human experience is about how the work environment ultimately impacts company performance, not just its culture. Our study shows that work places and work spaces have a key role to play, both

strategically and operationally, in fostering engagement, empowerment and fulfilment at work. JLL is on a journey of continuous innovation, and there are already many milestones and commitments to tech and innovation.

Practical takeaways checklist: top 10 tips

1 Many people have a distorted view of what AI can do. Ten to 15 years ago it simply wasn't a selling feature. Now, if you put an AI badge on anything, everyone wants it.

2 Many executives now realize that they are on a journey of continuous innovation.

3 AI technologies are changing rapidly, so businesses should consider having a platform that enables them to rapidly exploit these technologies rather than having lots of point solutions.

4 A start-up does not have the history and longevity of data. With reference to Gartner, a company might be a laggard in terms of their digital infrastructure, but they may not be laggards in terms of their depth of knowledge.

5 There is less risk to deploying AI today because we have data, the architecture to host it and the computer processing power at the right economic cost.

6 Regulation and the law are behind, but they are aware of it and they are catching up.

7 It is still unclear how AI will impact the morale of staff. A lot of AI solutions work in the background with no interference with humans as yet.

8 If you want to lead an industry, you need a transformational strategy. You need to think in the unknown and outside of the box.

9 When considering deploying AI, recognize the intrinsic motivation for many employees. Often the only relevant question is, 'what's in it for me?'

10 In sectors such as construction, robots currently are just glorified tools such as power drills or figures. We are nowhere near any sort of self-awareness or consciousness.

References

Accenture [accessed 9 July 2018] Oracle Technology Vision 2017, Accenture [Online] www.accenture.com/gb-en/insight-oracle-technlogy-vision-2017#maincontent-hero

JLL [accessed 25 September 2018] *Workplace: Powered by human experience, 2017* [Online] http://humanexperience.jll/global-report/

Juniper Research [accessed 12 June 2018] IoT Connections to Grow [Online] www.juniperresearch.com/press/press-releases/iot-connections-to-grow-140-to-hit-50-billion

Raconteur [accessed 9 July 2018] A Glimpse of the Future of Human Resources, Raconteur [Online] www.raconteur.net/business/glimpse-of-the-future-human-resources

Wadlow, T (2017) $27bn of Service Robots Will Be Sold During 2018–2020, IFR, 12/10 [Online] www.gigabitmagazine.com/ai/27bn-service-robots-will-be-sold-during-2018-2020-ifr

Transformational 05 marketing and AI in North America

Case studies from banking and retail

In this chapter we consider the impact of AI on both the banking and retail sectors, with a focus on North America, as well as examples from the UK.

AI in marketing is like teenage sex: marketers talk excitedly about it, but nobody really knows how to do it. Marketers convince themselves that everyone else is doing it, so everyone claims they are. Look no further than social platforms such as Twitter or LinkedIn and you will find global marketers across the ecosystem, furiously pimping their often-nebulous wares with a deluge of repetitive, cut and paste AI in marketing focused content. The reality is that many people are only just starting to take a punt with investment in AI for marketing. Also, by and large, it is in areas of relatively low value and non-core competence, akin to the way in which many companies offshored and outsourced their non-core services in the 1990s. This fever is gripping CMOs and their fellow board members across all sectors, including retail.

In the retail sector, the term AI is tossed around confusingly and interchangeably with other buzzwords such as digital transformation, agile, lean, digital, to name just a few. There is often limited understanding of what these terms mean. From a management and HR perspective, it is a traditional sector where many of those in senior positions typically do not come from a digital background; and one where you do your time as a buyer and slowly climb the corporate ladder. There is certainly a lot of hype linked to Amazon fever and a fear driving the need to 'keep up with the Jones'. There is a sense that there is digital trickery and an obsession with not being left behind.

Joel Edmondson is a former management consultant who now works in Dotcom at M&S, a major British multinational retailer headquartered in London. Established in 1884, M&S is listed on the London Stock Exchange and is a constituent of the FTSE 100 Index. Edmondson is leading an internal M&S start-up called Try Tuesday, an online womenswear personal styling service. He believes that customers now are craving a personal interaction, following years of dealing with automated customer-service systems.

No current retailers are winning because of AI in isolation right now. Two examples are ASOS and Primark. ASOS is the undisputed darling of British retail right now and is far ahead of the tech game. But you need to delve deep and analyse why they are performing. Is it AI or is it because they have a very good business proposition? Then take a good look at Primark, the current best performing clothing retailer. Their business model is one of the oldest in the world, premised on low price. Walk into any Primark store and you find people buzzing around, frantically filling their trolley to the absolute brim. At its core, shopping is a sociable hobby and one that will guard the place of a chain on the high street for many years to come.

In the short term, Edmondson believes that the likely impact of AI in marketing in retail will be the low hanging fruit. These are the numerical parts of the job, traditionally seen as number driven and typically outsourced to agencies. Examples include performance marketing and decisions on how to invest on Facebook. These are tasks that AI can now compute faster and better than humans. Another is web merchandising, which often sits inside marketing. AI-embedded tools can now be charged with this task and deliver great outcomes.

The personalization paradox

The third area is retail promotions, which is beginning to leave the human marketer out in the cold. The role of AI in personalization is enabling promotions to be targeted so precisely, such that you would never target someone who would not have bought the product anyway. Promotions are quite central to marketing's role in retail. On the trading floor, the only real lever marketing has in the short term, other than turning on more Facebook advertising, is to run another promotion. But crucial decisions need to be made. Does a 20 per cent discount look distressed? Should the marketer target top customers or just loyalty customers? AI is now making these central trading decisions.

So what is the future role of a merchandiser? Edmondson believes that this role could be overtaken by AI. So much of their job, for example allocation, how many to buy etc, simply won't be required to be done by a human brain any more. Instead they will learn which buttons to press on a computer. Which begs the question, what is the long-term future of marketing?

Are we witnessing a reversal?

In the 1980s, marketing was often centred around the big campaigns favoured by Don Draper in the Netflix hit series *Mad Men*. One of the protagonists in this fictional 1960s advertising agency, Draper has an ability to understand what pushes the emotional buttons of his clients. It leads him to recommend major campaigns that secure results. We often read how marketing is such a creative function, requiring imaginative thinking, and that this will spare the marketer from replacement by robots. But algorithms now allow computers to think intuitively. Netflix itself is a great example, as it analyses our viewing habits and now recommends similar viewing options.

Marketing 2.0 was a very different world. We moved away from a focus on the big marketing campaign; away from the emotion and awareness, to arguably a very functional, scientific marketing role that was for many simply too numeric and too heavily focused on proving the return on investment. As Edmondson explains: 'Take a giant step back and look at the 2000s, which were full of the big data revolution. Companies didn't succeed just because of big data'.

For AI to totally transform how things are done in retail, brands like Boohoo and Misguided could in theory take over the market and become number one. How quickly would that knowledge and insight filter to the big brands. How quickly would brands like Next, M&S, Debenhams then get behind this? There is evidence that it is happening but not at the pace some claim:

- In the next one to three years we will see a proof of concept phase. Some winners will be using AI and proving it can work.

- Years three to five are where fast followers will get involved and will start to use it in a way to meaningfully change how they do things.

- Years 5 to 10 are when the world of retail could look very different indeed.

Today's retail customers are migrating onto Dotcom for a plethora of reasons. Traditional retailers have too much excess square footage and need to think and act differently. But they can't get rid of their store estate quickly enough; they can't shed big costs; they can't take on the further burden of AI-related management overheads. So, they need to find smarter ways to do things. We are witnessing more of a push to AI than a pull from AI. A seamless customer journey is what everyone claims their customers want. If something is seamless, it isn't that memorable. This is actually where AI can help. The computer can know I'm about to go on your website and order socks. Put socks there; click one checkout and be done. Or do I want something a bit more memorable? In that sphere AI is a bit more unproven right now.

Try Tuesday is looking to use AI to assist in human relationships at scale. Retail has gone from a personal relationship to one where tech took over and now to one where tech assists. It will start by assisting. You will have people who are controlling the machines, and if they don't like the answer they will ignore it. But over time, as cost pressure increases in the market, it will be replaced. There will always be a bit of the customer craving a person. There is a whole industry in consulting that is 60 per cent founded on the basis of senior management not having access to the data they need. And many don't trust people below them. So they rely on consultants to come in and give an impartial view of their data. In a data-driven world, that goes away so you see another industry being disrupted and going away.

What does this mean for the high street in the future? At its heart, shopping is a social activity. It's a hobby for a lot of people. It's not a task on a 'To Do' list. This leads a lot of people to think in the future it's all about sexy, expensive stores that are super visual and cost a fortune. There are economic benefits in centralizing the distribution rather than going to everyone's house. At its heart it's quite an inefficient model not least in a world where we move away from peak stuff to experience. Personalization is a double-edged sword. If you get it wrong, you can really upset people. If you get it a bit, you make a lot of people a little bit happier. Personalization has often gone wrong in clothing. Take the example of someone who buys clothes for their mum who is plus-sized. Because that's in your data and the retailer doesn't know that you were buying for your mum, you keep getting spammed with plus-size info. They can reconcile why it's happened, but as a customer you may be really upset and put off by it. It's important to ask the question of how important seamlessness is. If we are channelling AI to solve problems, we need to be clear that we are solving the right problems.

Next, we turn our attention to a US restaurant chain as we hear from Sherif Mityas, Chief Experience Officer, TGI Fridays:

> From my perspective AI is really the fourth industrial revolution. It is going to transform how we think, what we do and how we interact; from our perspective internally as an organization, as well as externally with our guests. I know there is a lot of discussion, fear and hype around how AI is going to be the end of the worker, but I don't believe that. I believe that AI is going to help individuals be better at what they do. AI should be thought of as augmented intelligence. It really transforms because we have limited bandwidth as individuals. We can only take in so much; we can only look at so much and everyone wants us to focus. When you focus on something, you are better at it. When you become too broad and too scattered, by definition you are usually not deep enough and detailed enough to make the right decision at the right time. So by providing this augmented intelligence, with this digital assistant, you are automating those things that should be automated

Figure 5.1   TGI Fridays: digital platform and ordering capability on a mobile app

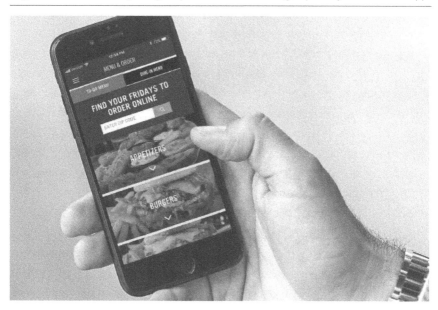

(Figure 5.1). You are allowing an individual to see what the next best decision is at the right time; that's the value. It's allowing that all the way up from the CEO of a board, to a doctor and other similar highly skilled positions, right down to a server at a restaurant. It's the ability to have a different, more meaningful, more efficient and effective interaction and work output, because you have the help and the help happens to be a machine.

We are in the hospitality business. Hospitality means you have to smile; you're trying to get to know that guest when they walk in. You are trying to understand why they are there; you are trying to engage and to make someone feel special when they walk into a restaurant as if you're inviting him [*sic*] into your home. We will absolutely be able to afford both machine and human, because the technology is going to become more affordable, and from a value perspective, it's more important to have it. It's not going to be a question of can you afford it. It will be that you have to afford it. Imagine that hostess having an earpiece wearable in the ear, and that guest walks in and you know, because of their mobile phone and past interactions, their name, their favourite drink, that their child has had a birthday last week. Imagine that interaction now. When you walk in and are greeted by name; they ask you if you want your favourite drink and go on to tell you it's actually ready for you at the bar and then congratulate you on your wedding anniversary last week.

To me there are two pieces of AI. There is the AI that can automate things and create efficiency; they can do a lot of things to make things faster but to me that is only half the story. If we only use AI in that regard, we are missing the true capabilities, which is how do you create better interaction or loyalty with your end consumers because you know more. You can personalize the experience and differentiate for them. That creates loyalty, that creates frequency, and that differentiates you.

Some people will be freaked by this; there is no question. With all the dialogue about sharing of data and how we are using our data, we have found that if you are upfront with the consumer and tell them, yes I'm collecting your data, but here is how I'm going to use it. I'm going to use it because I think you will want your favourite drink to be at the bar when you walk in. I think you'd want me to fill your cart every Tuesday because I know it's soccer night and you want to pick up food for the family. So if I can do something to make it easier or more convenient or more personal, we actually get guests saying yes, let me opt in. Yes I want to give you this data so that you can give me something more valued back in return.

We still need good marketing talent. You still need art; you still need that experience; you still need people that are creative from a marketing perspective. But again if I can make that great marketing person more effective through the addition of something like AI and technology, why wouldn't you do that? From a competitive perspective, everybody is trying to secure the guest. In this sector we are done with segments and micro segments and with baby boomers. We are done with lookalikes. I need to know who Jane is vs John. The only way you're going to do that is to balance the art and science of marketing.

For us there are real ROI-driven AI projects happening. We are seeing real benefits for example, making your restaurant more efficient using AI. This means giving those tools to managers to be able to do things like staff better, order food better, reduce fraud and waste better; so using machine learning we can help our restaurant run more efficiently. We have done a lot of that in-house. A lot of the things we have built are in-house.

We are able to use AI to again personalize our marketing; such as how, when and where we interact with a guest. We have been able to drive a doubling over our online business through personalization in less than 12 months. We have engaged with guests 300 per cent more on our social platforms, because we are able to have individual conversations and there we use a host of different people. Everything from Conversible, who are a great partner, and they power our AI chatbots. Also Facebook, Twitter, Amazon Alexa. We also then have a group called Amperity, which helps us to stitch the data, John vs Mary and then how do we touch them, and then how that content goes back out to groups like Urban Airship and some of those other channels. So we use a lot of partners – another is Hypergiant – because it's the new frontier and there's lots of things you have to worry about all the data and all the ways that you can touch someone. It is also changing so fast that by definition I want to have new people come in and tell us what's next. So we have different projects to keep us relevant and in front.

I think the more forward, leading edge use cases are definitely going to be more Asia, China led. They are going to be the ones who are more doing all the facial recognition, understanding who this person is by actually taking the 40 points around their face, and that is already out there. There are restaurants, where you walk in and stare at the screen and you can pay for your meal. I think where AI is going to grow fast here in the West is where it is not as in your face. People talking to Alexa don't view that as AI. My children use Alexa; they consider her like a sister; they ask her questions; she tells them bedtime stories; they don't think of it as oh this is an AI thing, it's Alexa. It's a little assistant someone who tells us the weather and plays music.

It's almost coming full circle. We started with phones that we spoke to, and then we went to phones that we use our thumbs on. Now we are going back to devices where we talk to them again. It's amazing because the next generation is growing up just talking to things, and that's how they think now. That's how they operate. People are not going to think of them as robots, or AI and machines. It's literally like part of the conversation, and it's natural to have these conversations with things around us. We are going to be talking to our cars; we're going to be talking to refrigerators. It's going to be part of our normal day. But it's not going to be this Terminator robot taking over the world.

We are allowing the machine to create contact and so it has to be in our brand voice. We have to teach the machine how to talk in Friday's; to have fun and be social but not rude. You need to be able to teach the machine to have a certain vernacular, and so you teach it like you would an infant. You teach it where the boundaries are and when it goes outside of that, you kind of slap it back. But you have to go through that learning process; the learning process happens on both sides. The technology has to learn, but the organization also has to learn as well, and if either one gets out of line, that's when you get trouble.

I do feel positive about it. My children are growing up with it; it's not scary to them. They don't see Alexa as this scary device sitting on the countertop because it makes things fun to them. It makes things easier. They talk to something and it plays their favourite song. To me it's just going to happen. I think we are going to look back and just say what were we worried about?

With any new technology, there are going to be things that are too far out there. People are going to try things because it sounds interesting, but it's just not going to make sense. We have failed on a couple of things but that's the whole beauty of it. Like with anything new and innovative, there are going to be things that you fail at, but to us it is a learning opportunity so we a) don't do it again and b) we learn from it.

Next we hear from Olin Novak, former Chief Marketing Officer for retail giant Tesco in Central Europe. Tesco is a UK multinational groceries and general merchandise retailer. Novak comments:

When it comes to fourth generation tools such as AI, it is actually the IT teams who are usually the experts. He believes that CMOs don't care that much how AI can be used or what the benefits are. They are focused on like for like, budgets and communications, as opposed to change and making huge progress with clients ... Many retailers have limited capital investment, so they decide what needs to be done first.

Consequently, Novak predicts that the major companies in retail will find it really difficult, and that change will come from start-ups or those who started online and were able to include this architecture and AI in what they do on a daily basis.

It's much easier for start-ups and smaller companies to innovate. If you start something from scratch, it's much easier to develop it so it fits the current world. For the major players, the capital expenditure (capex) would be significant, and the risk of failure is sometimes too big. Big companies try to innovate and take small steps but are often hindered by the mindset and culture of the company.

Another major obstacle is that in large traditional companies, there is often still a battle to secure and retain the largest teams and biggest budgets. But this works contra to the progress you can make with AI, which can be focused on saving time and resources; being more accurate; providing better quality and making it cheaper.

According to Novak, 'This goes against many C level directors' objectives. Ego can play a major part as those managers still want to run huge complex teams. As a result, the only way for the bigger animals to succeed is to buy these smaller businesses'.

Pressure comes mainly from smaller companies who are growing fast as a result of their investment in AI. Top and bottom line is important for them to deliver, but there are different ways for them to deliver it. For 30 years, many of these companies have delivered it a certain way, so it will be incredibly difficult for them to change.

But time is not on their side. AI is already here and is already impacting businesses. Some are working with it better than others. Going forward, the importance of working out how AI can be helpful will be strengthening, and the changes will happen more and more quickly. Each and every year it will be more and more important. In the retail space, Novak believes that once someone in the industry does something broader and bigger than the others, the rest will just follow.

Novak believes that marketing is crucial when it comes to AI's success in the retail arena: 'A lot of people think AI is first and foremost about making things and processes cheaper. That should be a side effect. The first thing marketers should consider is making customers happy and more satisfied. Do this and they will love you'.

Major retailers are also putting technological solutions to the test:

By combining vending machines with artificial intelligence, Coca-Cola intends to bring more joy to the purchase of a sugary drink. Vending machines will be able to chat in a two-way conversation, building emotional connections between Coke and consumers.

While confectionery giant, Mars, is using 'emotional intelligence' – an application of computer vision and machine learning – to gauge facial reactions to product marketing after finding that positive face expressions could predict advertisements with high sales impacts. Kellogg's and Coca-Cola are reportedly also using the technology to optimize their product marketing.

Smart shopping trolleys, equipped with barcode scanners and locating technology, have started to hit retail stores around the world, including in Australia. [… Or] what if [shopping] trolleys were also equipped with resistance controls to incorporate physical activity into your daily shop, with personalized and tailored nutritious food marketing? […] We could capitalize on retail digital shelf technology to display not only pricing and nutritional information, but also farm-to-fork traceability of foods at point of purchase, and complementary healthy food marketing (Backholer, 2018).

All of the above shows the enormous scope that AI can have in the retail sector, not only in terms of creating a more positive and enjoyable customer experience but also in the wider impact that it can have on our health.

A report by McKinsey and Company confirms the role that AI can play in the retail industry, as it suggests:

The business areas that traditionally provide the most value to companies tend to be the areas where AI can have the biggest impact. In retail organizations, for example, marketing and sales has often provided significant value… While applications of AI cover a full range of functional areas, it is in fact in these two cross-cutting ones – supply-chain management/manufacturing and marketing and sales – where we believe AI can have the biggest impact, at least for now, in several industries. Combined, we estimate that these use cases make up more than two-thirds of the entire AI opportunity. AI can create $1.4–$2.6 trillion of value in marketing and sales across the world's businesses and $1.2–$2 trillion in supply chain management and manufacturing (some of the value accrues to companies while some is captured by customers).

(Chui, Henker and Miremadi, 2018)

[Kroger, one of America's largest grocery chains] has decided to embrace technology to help it survive and thrive in the 4th industrial revolution.

With 2,782 grocery stores under nearly two dozen names in 35 states, Kroger plans to leverage its data, shopper insights and scale to help it remain a leader in the marketplace of the future. The grocer already delivers 3 billion personalized recommendations each year, but they will enhance the personalization efforts to create different experiences for customers. Not only will shoppers receive useful content digitally but also 'inspiration' through product-related content and recipes.

Today, we can get groceries delivered, but Kroger is testing the delivery of the future – grocery delivery by an autonomous vehicle. Kroger partnered with Nuro, a Silicon Valley company that specializes in autonomous vehicles for delivery, on its pilot program.

[Furthermore] a partnership between Kroger and British online-only grocer Ocado is expected to help Kroger automate its warehouses and use artificial intelligence to bolster its bottom line. Ocado claims to have the world's most sophisticated automated grocery warehouses and has worked with Uber and Instacart to test delivery options, and it's this know-how that Kroger aims to leverage with its investment. Ocado's warehouses are run by robots that are powered by machine learning algorithms to navigate around the warehouse and pick products for orders. With this investment and access to Ocado's technology, Kroger will get products to stores more efficiently.

(Marr, 2018)

Dilemma for CMOs: knowing where to turn

There are huge challenges ahead for CMOs. For starters, it's impossible for them to sort the wheat from the chaff and decide who can offer the right solutions to progress further. For example, some masquerade as AI suppliers when in actual fact they are simply offering automation tools. If you meet all the potential suppliers, you get nothing done. If you don't meet any, you don't learn enough and know what the opportunities are. Novak advises CMOs to pull in the right experts. But first, they need to truly understand how it can fit their operating model and how they can simplify the way their teams are working. Part of the problem is that many senior managers are not even experts in how their companies operate.

From a marketing perspective, Novak believes that the future is in image, text and voice recognition. But the key is how to deploy it in a business. With image recognition you can learn how to execute in a store. AI can show where the mistakes are. Then people in the stores can make the changes. But if 80 per cent of the stores are not executing it properly, then most likely it is too difficult for them or there are other fundamental issues that need to be addressed. How to take great ideas and turn them into something tangible and cost effective is not as easy as it sounds and requires commitment and the collaboration of the whole board.

A future of self-regulation

Novak has children aged 10 and 12 and believes that the new generation will have a very different approach, one that will sort out the ethics debate. He believes that people in the West in their thirties to sixties focus on being wealthy, travelling, eating better food and having better experiences. His optimistic outlook is that the new generation is more relaxed about those things and will be more focused on doing the right things and on being helpful, particularly in Western Europe where they have enough money by and large and are heavily influenced by social media. 'When they are economically active, they will have very different views on where they spend their money, where they go, who they buy from. They will vote with their feet. In less developed markets, they want more success and it will take a few more generations'.

In his fascinating book, *Why AI Hallucinates: The BotVerse Begins* (2018), Mike Duke, Chief Innovation Architect, Wells Fargo, explains:

> Financial services will dramatically change as machine learning moves transactional costs lower than ever before and time to market is exponentially reduced for new products and services. The question we need to ask is, which aspects of work won't be impacted by AI? As efficiencies are realized by AI for redundant activities, proactive strategies will be reclaimed by human leaders in the organization. In terms of a framework for success, companies need to take the following five steps:

1 Identify activities best solved by AI

2 Develop transition plans

3 Install oversight and efficiency monitors (humans)

4 Execute

5 Repeat.

In an interview conducted in March 2018 with AI Business, Duke continues: 'The financial services sector is one of the core adopters of AI, largely thanks to the sheer volume of data fuelling the sector. Beyond algorithmic trading, though, financial services firms have a keen interest in AI for a number of reasons'. Duke argues that AI is beneficial for financial services not only from a security perspective but also for providing a comprehensive contextual understanding of customers, which can benefit all businesses:

> Whether it's B2B or B2C, we feel that AI is a great opportunity to improve security paradigms exponentially. These firms are also looking at this space in order to get closer to their customers' specific needs. I've talked to a lot of fintech and financial services firms who, quite honestly, are jealous of the understanding that Google has of its users... We believe that a better understanding of the behaviour and transactional activities of our customers will empower us to protect their assets and their financial futures.
>
> Small, medium and large businesses all have one thing in common. They want to get closer to their customers and understand their needs, and we feel like AI is going to get us closer to that. Any product or service out there that has anything to do with AI is going to come back to these core features. Knowing who you're talking to, knowing who your AI is working with, and allowing your AI to build a better contextual understanding of who your customer is.

Ultimately, Duke believes AI is going to enable the restoration of truly personal relationships with consumers:

> Back in the door-knocking days, if you were selling cable TV, you could ask customers what they want to watch. You could customize it. That... personal relationship with customers is a lost art. Ironically, it's going to take this new version of technology to return us to that.

That'll be the magical gift of artificial intelligence. Not just a greater understanding of what customers need today, but what they're going to need tomorrow. The person that solves this problem will be on top of the world, because that gets us back to what a real customer relationship used to be.

(AI Business, 2018)

Digital workplaces

Let's look at this in practice learning from the marketing department at Konica Minolta Business Solutions Europe. We spoke to Olaf Lorenz, General Manager of their International Marketing Division:

In the last decade, workplaces have started to evolve towards digitalization. In the future people will work in digitally connected environments where personalization is enabled, collaboration, data sharing and information management are automated.

Ultimately, these future workplaces will provide artificial intelligence (AI) and decision support that leverage both localized information and broader community knowledge whenever needed. Such digital workplaces will rely on the availability of data and on the ability to analyse and produce meaningful and valuable insight from it. The emergence of AI, combined with deep learning technologies and new business models, is already enabling Konica Minolta to manage information flows in these digital workplaces. Within the marketing sector AI can help to reinvent existing products and services to enhance new user experiences and making more personalized marketing techniques possible. AI will set a new level of user experience in the near future, so marketers will need to deliver against this increase in customer expectations.

Collaboration

For AI to be effective, we need to create more collaborative, socially oriented and communicative systems that interact with individual employees and groups in a more structured way. We also need to build a supporting digital environment in which AI can navigate and operate separately and together in clusters. The challenge is to start creating information points within organizations that can exploit AI in a more social setting, to influence shared intelligence in small groups and promote collective knowledge sharing throughout the entire business. Therefore, influencer marketing might be the first area impacted here, as AI and predictive technology will help both customers and marketers to get closer to each other.

History has repeatedly shown us, through automation, as people and technologies advance, [that] there are new jobs being created rather than being destroyed. In the past technology has always ended up creating more jobs because of the way automation works in practice. In automating a particular task so that it can be done more quickly or cheaply, [this] leads to an increase in the demand for human workers to do the other tasks around it that have not been automated, giving us more time for creativity and innovation. We believe there should be a transition period from the traditional approach of engineering AI to one that ultimately results in the generation of self-organization. This is a challenging transition that will play a significant part in the evolution towards a true AI, which will unleash an intuitive understanding of the workplace and will enable employees to make better decisions about their organization, colleagues and workplace.

Evidence-based marketing

Konica Minolta is exploring how to generate evidence-based business services, which address the axes of workplace efficiency and effectiveness. Our developments focus on the value of data being generated by new sensing devices, which form a real-time flow of workplace data which will soon connect to analytical and cognitive platforms. They make our workplaces more secure, effective and more adaptive to specific groups or individual needs and help organizations generate new insights, which help govern workplace environments.

Konica Minolta's Workplace Hub, the world's most connected intelligent edge platform, for the Workplace of The Future, is an innovative new enterprise IT solution that unifies all of an organization's technology via a single centralized platform.

The platform's product roadmap includes future integration of IoT, Artificial Intelligence, Intelligent Edge and Decision Support capabilities as they become more central to the business environment. Adding this cognitive layer of organizational insight unleashes an intuitive understanding of the world that empowers people to collaborate more and to make smarter, data-driven decisions more effectively and easily. Ultimately, we are helping in turning the tsunami of information into meaningful data assisting clients, making the right business decisions and work life more effective.

In order to build truly empowering AI, it is fundamental to take a broad perspective that builds a digital environment and enables digital intelligence to flourish. This means adopting the following:

- to build AI platforms that are based on the laws of complexity and exploit approaches that are linked to natural evolutionary models;
- to evolve any existing cloud infrastructures;
- to use the Internet of Things as a consistent platform to create an interface that could work like a digital membrane in a physical world.

Creating basic systems following these principles will bring companies closer to the moment in which more of our world can be better understood and even predicted.

Redefining the rules of restaurant management

Helen Vaid, Chief Global Customer Officer for Pizza Hut and one of the keynote speakers at The AI Customer Summit comments, 'A lot of time in your business, you tend to follow certain assumptions, whereas someone who doesn't have the same overhead can sometimes come in and question things you don't. We'd love to see what the new technologies are and how they are looking to redefine the rules of restaurant management'.

Practical takeaways checklist: top 10 tips

1 AI in marketing is like teenage sex: marketers talk excitedly about it, but nobody really knows how to do it.

2 The role of AI in personalization is enabling promotions to be targeted so precisely, such that you would never target someone who would not have bought the product anyway.

3 Personalization is a double-edged sword. If you get it wrong, you can really upset people.

4 AI is going to help individuals be better at what they do. AI should be thought of as augmented intelligence.

5 AI can make a great marketing person more effective; it enables you to balance the art and science of marketing.

6 As with anything new and innovative, there are going to be things that you fail at with AI. It's crucial to treat it as a learning opportunity.

7 As efficiencies are realized by AI for redundant activities, proactive strategies will be reclaimed by human leaders in the organization.

8 History shows us that through automation, as people and technologies advance, new jobs are created, rather than destroyed.

9 For AI to be effective, we need to create more collaborative, socially oriented and communicative systems that interact with individual employees and groups in a more structured way.

10 Be aware that some companies masquerade as AI suppliers when in actual fact they simply offer automation tools but with an AI tag.

References

AI Business [accessed 9 July 2018] Modern AI Means A Collaborative Universe of Bots – Interview with Wells Fargo Chief Innovation Architect, 01/03 [Online] https://aibusiness.com/mike-duke-wells-fargo/

Backholer, K [accessed 23 July 2018] We Must Ensure New Food Retail Technologies Are Pathways – Not Barriers – to Better Health. The Independent, 14/07 [Online] www.independent.co.uk/life-style/gadgets-and-tech/food-retail-technology-amazon-google-deliveroo-health-diet-a8419726.html

Chui, M, Henker, N and Miremadi, M [accessed 23 July 2018] Most of AI's Business Uses Will Be in Two Areas. Harvard Business Review, 20/07 [Online] https://hbr.org/2018/07/most-of-ais-business-uses-will-be-in-two-areas?utm_campaign=hbr&utm_source=twitter&utm_medium=social\

Duke, M (2018) *Why AI Hallucinates: The BotVerse Begins*, 1st edn, United States of America, Global Innovation Books

Marr, B [accessed 23 July 2018] Forbes, 20/07 [Online] www.forbes.com/sites/bernardmarr/2018/07/20/how-us-retail-giant-kroger-is-using-ai-and-robots-to-prepare-for-the-4th-industrial-revolution/#59fc69b217d6

Transformational 06 marketing and AI in technology and venture capital

With a special focus on the Middle East

In this chapter we delve deeply into the world of AI in the technology sector. As we move around the globe, we also focus our attention on the Middle East. There is a huge push for AI and emerging technology in this part of the world, specifically in the United Arab Emirates (UAE). It's no surprise, given PwC's predictions that the potential impact of AI for this region will be US $320 billion. Endless opportunities await, because 'AI has the potential to fundamentally disrupt markets in the Middle East through the creation of innovative new services and entirely new business models. We've already seen the impact of the first wave of digitization. With the eruption of AI, some of the market leaders in ten, even five years' time may be companies you've never heard of' (PwC, 2018b). AI is certainly at the forefront of the UAE government's strategic plans. As part of its strategy for AI and its commitment towards technological enhancement, HH Sheikh Mohammed Bin Rashid Al Maktoum, Vice President and Prime Minister of the UAE and Ruler of Dubai, appointed HE Omar Bin Sultan Al Olama as the first Minister of State for AI.

According to Phil Mennie, Technology and Digital Risk Director at PwC Middle East, some companies in the region are mandated to adopt AI. It is pushed down from above, and there is both the money and incredible ambition for technology:

This industrial revolution is like nothing seen before. It's not limited to AI; IoT, blockchain, robotics, AR, VR will all cause major disruption by 2030. AI is forecast to contribute $15.7 trillion to the economy and it's easy to see how. Every day there is a new AI start-up, and they are excellent at marketing their AI products. Today, computing power is really cheap, and due to all of the sensors, we have massive amounts of data. The United Arab Emirates (the UAE) wants to be at the forefront of technology. AI is a real hot topic across the globe at the moment with a lot of investment going into it. But the heightened expectations about AI have led to a number of misconceptions about exactly what it can do. I've been spending time with clients to help them define their ambitions for AI and understand what they need to achieve them. To do this, we use PwC's Responsible AI framework to help address the key risks and issues that clients face, and I've recently taken [on] the role of Responsible AI leader for the Middle East. I spoke at Dubai's AI and Cognitive Computing Conference recently on the topic of 'Safeguarding AI' and it was great to see about how much interest I got from companies across a wide range of industries.

Mennie does not believe that AI is making a huge impact on marketing today, because the technology is currently driving it: 'In marketing, everyone is doing a lot of clever data analytics. It's unclear whether many have learning algorithms and actual AI. I also don't understand the hype around chatbots, which have been around for ages. But the potential is huge, for example, AI being able to serve the customer with relevant adverts'.

Another leading consultancy firm is KPMG. One of their recent surveys sheds light on the belief in the potential for AI to expand businesses:

Some 88 per cent of tech CEOs surveyed by KPMG said they were confident in their growth potential for their companies over the next three years. More than half – 52 per cent, to be precise – said they expected their companies to grow by at least 2 per cent a year over that time period. That's more optimistic than CEOs as a whole. Overall, 44 per cent of CEOs said they expected their firms to grow 2 per cent annually over the next three years.

(Wolverton, 2018)

Sticking with KPMG, we now turn to Samer M. Abdallah, PhD, who is Head of Digital Transformation at KPMG in Saudi Arabia. He explains:

> From a business point of view, people are asking about AI. They are trying to better understand and discover what AI is, what does it mean to their business, and how this may disrupt their business models. Is AI really a risk for the business or is it more of an opportunity?
>
> On the other hand, there are those who are engaged in developing AI-based solutions. There is a race on as to who will crack the code on various aspects of AI, and this involves the major and obvious players, including IBM, Microsoft, Google, Amazon, Facebook. Many niche players are also trying to solve specific problems of AI.
>
> What we have seen in the last 18 months is a culmination of the efforts over the last 20 years. We were doing some interesting work back in the 1990s, but the commercialization was not possible due to the high tag price of development, and because the computational power wasn't strong enough. It would take you days, if not weeks, to train neural network systems to do anything meaningful. The instrumentation and sensors were very expensive; computation power and data storage … [were] very expensive. What's making things now possible is the drop in price of all of those things, but more importantly, the connectivity of all of those things (Internet of Things – IoT) and the public solicitation of data very freely. As individuals, we are really giving away data very freely every time we go on mobile phones or the internet. This abundance of data is making AI possible.

What is making connectivity possible?

It is the sensors and IoT that also adapt and mean we can connect the dots to better understand our customers and even predict their behaviours in particular situations. We are always leaving some digital trace behind. Companies collecting our data can therefore track our movements, purchases, chats on social media and preferences. It is connecting all the dots and the data that relates to the same persona; so it is building the story around us. This is making us visible and also our preferences and needs visible, so companies can target us with bespoke marketing to sell us something at the right time and place. This connectivity is key; for example, your car connects to your phone, which in turn connects to the dealer and the manufacturer.

So connectivity is really the immersion of the human and the machine, with the data flowing between them. This means you can really build a story about a person with data analytics and AI. This means that you can target people with the right type of marketing or technology.

The level of adoption of AI varies among countries. In certain geographies, there will still be further exploration in the next 18 months, and there will be exponential adoption in more mature geographies, especially where data is available and connectivity is high. We will see major AI-based solutions made by the major players and even new niche players. At the same time, there will be some dampening of some of the hype that has happened around AI. I think people will start to understand and be more realistic about what it can do over the next five years. I think this differentiation between what is real and what is hype is going to happen over the next 18 months as consumers begin to understand more. Those people that are developing AI have played a bit of a marketing stunt over the last 18 months to put themselves on the map. Knowingly or not knowingly they have caused the hype. Now the delivery is going to prove problematic in certain areas so they might start focusing on what can actually be delivered in the near future.

Will AI just be seen as computer software?

In general, many of the big players sell you a box of APIs, with a development environment to implement particular AI solutions. Many of the APIs are open source. Some niche players are focusing their effort on providing a solution to a particular business problem. At KPMG we have, for example, Ignite that is based on the same concept, where we have a development platform with a suite of APIs. We do as well develop solutions for specific business problems. While some of our solutions are helping KPMG transform its own business, the majority of our solutions are designed to help our clients transform their businesses. Many major players like Google, Amazon and Facebook are employing data analytics and AI algorithms at the core of their own business model to get insights and drive value from the data they are collecting on the users of their platforms. How do I do marketing using AI is a big question. How do I target my customers, to sell the right product of service, at the right time and at the right place?

We have seen major alliances being forged among companies to provide solutions. For example, KPMG have alliances with Google, Microsoft and IBM, where KPMG provide the in-depth business knowledge, and the technology companies provide the technical advancement. The result is growth for both parties and accelerated AI solutions to the market.

Predicting customer needs

The use of data analytics, at least in its predictive form, and more recently AI, is more prevalent in the marketing function than any other function. This is mainly due to the availability of data that companies have been collecting on their customers for many years. Data analytics and AI marketing solutions exist and are provided by many players in the market. All thanks to availability of customer data and the high connectivity, we can now predict when a customer needs a particular product before they place an order and 'wow them' by delivering it. A car company can predict that a particular client is about to change their 5-year-old car and switching to another brand and target them with the right offer so that [sic] not to lose them.

The repercussions of AI are scary in the longer term, but in the short to medium term I am not so concerned. I don't think we are producing smart enough machines to be scared and I think we are safe for now. It is right, however, to be scared of the potential malicious use of the technology. AI can be utilized for good or bad intentions. Of course hackers can use it in a very bad way. For example, at my smarthome I have technology that I can control from anywhere in the world. A hacker could access this and open my door and access my home or the cameras, and this is scary. Because of the connectivity, cyber-attacks are also a real concern. The moment you start connecting things and have a flow of data, people can use it in a bad way.

The GDPR regulations that came out in Europe are going to regulate and force companies to behave a certain way when it comes to data. In the short to medium term, I am more afraid of the misuse of data or the cyber-attacks to break down particular systems or even security systems or military systems that can have major repercussions. But in [the] longer term and with the advance of quantum computing, the potential of AI applications will grow exponentially and so will the potential of misuse of such technology. The intelligence that a machine can have and the 'self-learning' potential of machines can't be underestimated. Then it becomes quite scary in terms of the implications of how it could 'misbehave'. There is a debate now regarding regulations. Can I trust the outcome of an AI system if I cannot reverse engineer how the AI system arrived at such an outcome? Theoretically, you can trace a decision back to what has happened, but it is not practically possible and some people are just discussing it. If I can't trace it, I can't trust it. This is a big debate, which might slow down innovation.

In my humble opinion, general artificial intelligence is something that we probably should not pursue and if you are pursuing it, it is not 2050; it's beyond that. I think we will have artificial intelligence that solves particular problems that they are trained to do but not general artificial intelligence for the foreseeable future.

In the foreseeable future, AI will be able to at best solve complex problems or augment human knowledge to make very complex decisions. This is limited to particular situations and functions which they will be trained to do. You can't just make them generally smart. Now aged 50, I can easily make inferences from a field of physics into a situation in life. I base this on the experiences in life that I can borrow from here and apply there and see analogies. However, AI is nowhere near this. We are intelligent because we can make connections and we can make jokes or bring things up that are not really related. I have to be philosophical here and say do we really want to create machines like this. I think that's the scary part of it. There needs to be ethics built around it. The cat is out of the bag now, so I don't think we can prevent development. If it can happen, it's going to happen. I don't think its 2050 though.

With regard to regulation, governments are slower than the private sector. The major players are trying to regulate their own work. It is never ideal given what you have seen happening with some of them regarding data breaches. It is never ideal, but the problem is the government does not understand enough about this topic to regulate against it or with it. AI could really be doing good for humanity, so we have to balance those needs. The standards don't exist and this is a problem.

At KPMG we recently interviewed global CEOs for a report called *Growing Pain*. We asked them to consider whether in the next three years they believe they will see an increase in the jobs related to AI. So there is research on the need for innovators, curators, data analytics and computer scientists, and AI programmers. These are very scarce skills, and universities need to take note of this as there are lots of courses online and people are reinventing themselves in this space. There is a shortage; so there will be losses of jobs, but it's not as massive as we think. For example, by 2025 there will be a big chunk of jobs that are mundane and repetitive. Many jobs, between 20 to 50 per cent, that fall under this criteria could disappear by 2025. Telephone operators are a good example. There may well be a loss of 30 per cent of phone operators' jobs because of voice recognition and language processing. AI can answer standard queries and many people are unsettled as they will lose their jobs. But far less so in the next three years.

With regard to the change in minimum wage, it is up to governments to plan and regulate. If we're talking about 2025, this is seven years down the track. However, this is seven years away. Training and re-skilling the workforce is possible for certain workforce segments.

There are ideas that are being floated about universal income. If I am 'employing a robot', will I be paying tax on robots? With robots you are making more money as a company so shouldn't you be taxed more for the deployment? So if you pay tax for those robots, you bridge some of the gap of unemployment by compensating those that are mostly affected. Universal income is a complicated problem to solve. What if you have American companies having call centres in the Philippines employing Philippine staff. But they are making more money for the US headquarters. Where is the universal income paid for the loss of jobs?

The customer is to a certain extent the voice of the employee who has lost his [sic] job because of the AI. Recently, we have been seeing a push back from the customer and from companies who do not look after the environment and push back on companies who don't have the proper gender equality or focus on employee wellbeing. Now with social media and globalization, any incident like this that might look unethical and affect the company becomes key.

Dubai and AI

Dubai has always been a city of pure excellence and has recently been dubbed the 'city of the future', thanks to its ambitions to become the world's leading smart hub. It is no surprise that Dubai is thus eager to embrace blockchain and AI as it rapidly transforms into a smart city and sets its sights on becoming the world's first blockchain-powered government. The first edition of the world-AI show will take place in this region in April 2019, as the UAE has put itself at the forefront of AI development with the announcement of a dedicated ministry for AI, and with Dubai Police implementing a fully functional robot police.

UAE Strategy for Artificial Intelligence

In October 2017, the UAE Government launched the following 'UAE Strategy for Artificial Intelligence (AI)' (UAE Government Portal, 2018). The AI strategy will cover the following sectors:

- Transport – to reduce accidents and cut operational costs
- Health – to minimize chronic and dangerous diseases
- Space – to help conduct accurate experiments and reduce the rate of costly mistakes
- Renewable energy – to manage facilities
- Water – to conduct analysis and studies to provide water sources
- Technology – to increase productivity and help with general spending
- Education – to cut costs and enhance desire for education
- Environment – to increase forestation rate
- Traffic – to reduce accidents and traffic jams and draw more effective traffic policies.

The AI strategy has five themes:

1 The formation of the UAE AI Council

2 Workshops, programmes, initiatives and field visits to government bodies

3 Develop capabilities and skills of all staff operating in the field of technology and organize training courses for government officials

4 Provide all services via AI and the full integration of AI into medical and security services

5 Launch leadership strategy and issue a government law on the safe use of AI.

In Dubai, the local government has launched its own roadmap for AI. A key project is an intelligent assistant called Rashid, launched in 2016 and built on IBM Watson technology. It was the first Dubai government service using AI, using natural language to understand citizens' requests for information. It is first being used to make it easier to set up businesses in the city. Entrepreneurs can ask Rashid questions on business licensing requirements and regulation processes, for instance, and get responses in real time, HE Aisha says.

The Office is now exploring the possibility of Rashid working across public and private sector services. 'It will become a "personal concierge" for people living in Dubai', she adds, 'helping us book flights, tickets, cabs, or even find the best schools for our children' (GovInsider, 2018).

UAE's Vice President and Prime Minister Shaikh Mohammad Bin Rashid Al Maktoum stated:

> Adaptation to advanced technologies and utilizing them in serving society and enhancing the efficiency of government performance is a firmly established approach adopted by the UAE.
>
> The Gulf city is also seeking to be safer along with being smarter as it aims to use artificial intelligence to police the emirate. The Brazil-headquartered security organization Polsec presented futuristic artificial intelligence camera and sensor technology that sees, smells and listens for potential problems, to delegates at the Future Cities Show at Dubai World Trade Center.
>
> (Forbes Middle East, 2018)

No chapter on technology would be complete without a focus on some of the leading tech players in the market today. So we now turn to Julien Simon, Principal Technical Evangelist, AI and Machine Learning at Amazon Web Services (AWS). He comments:

At AWS we have millions of customers and they come in all sizes and shapes, from individual developers, to governments and large enterprise[s] in every single segment, every single vertical. We therefore have a pretty extensive view of what's going on. Focusing on machine learning, all verticals and types of industries are looking at AI. Obviously, you have some leaders; FSI is an obvious one because obviously they have a lot of data and have had it for a long time. They have been working on machine learning for a long time already and have real-life problems to solve like fraud prevention and credit decisions, and not to mention pricing models for everything. So FSI is definitely leading the way. They are probably on the more sophisticated end of the machine learning spectrum – they have big teams and budgets so they don't necessarily need help with algorithms or on building models. They need help on scaling and running machine learning in the most agile and cost-efficient way. In a sense that is what AWS has been all about for 10 years; helping organizations to build agile and cost-effective and secure infrastructure. It's similar to what we have done for infrastructure in general with cloud computing.

We're building services that let those sophisticated machine learning users be more agile and be able to experiment faster with machine learning. Normal companies who have a very decent business and may have data or could grab data and could of course make their product or service larger by incorporating machine learning into it. Obviously, their skill levels and budget are different. The amount of time and energy they are ready to invest is different. So we also build high level services that are based on deep learning for let's say image recognition, video recognition, speech-text, chatbots etc. But clients don't have to worry about it. They just use APIs, as they have done with AWS for cloud infrastructure. If you want to process a real-time video stream and do object detection, then you just call an API and get it done and don't have to know the first thing about machine learning.

So we see early adopters or people who have been doing machine learning for decades who need to scale and don't want to spend huge amounts of money building physical infrastructure for machine learning and want to give their teams as much 'bang for the[ir] buck'. Here again FSI is up there, retail is up and maybe some other verticals are less advanced, but they will catch up at some point. And then we have start-ups or regular companies who think that they have relevant data and want to use it in the easiest and most cost-effective way possible to make their products and services scale. AWS is about democratizing technology, and again what we have built over the years when it comes to infrastructure, databases, storage etc, gives the ability to the individual developer or smaller start-up to compete globally with the same technology and weapons that the major players deploy.

AWS is about building blocks; we build the Lego blocks and they come in all sizes and shapes and colours. It's all pay as you go, so as long as you stay small scale you can experiment with the actual services at almost zero cost. They just use the AWS console and just use the services – if they like them they can scale them to the moon, if they don't they just paid a few dollars. We even have what we call the free tier, which is a way to use many AWS services for free for 12 months.

I have a good example. It's a solar panel company called PowerScout. If they were a traditional company you would think they would do marketing the usual way – send emails, send snail mail and try to get homeowners interested in their service etc. But they did something really different. They used satellite pictures of the areas they are interested in, and using deep learning, they actually located the houses that they thought were the best candidates for solar panel installation. Probably based on the size of the roof and orientation with respect to the sun – so by building and training a deep learning model to analyse those pictures – on AWS – they could identify the houses, and they would only target those.

GDPR is a gamechanger for marketing. I'm a customer and like everyone else I think spam is a nightmare and SMS is really painful and unwanted phone calls – and the sad thing is that I might have been interested in that product if it had been presented in a smart way, but if you cold call me at 8 pm while I'm having dinner or you spam me to death it gives me a negative view of your company and I won't do business with you. People are getting more and more educated and becoming more aware of those techniques, so they are resisting more as well. So marketing and advertising in general needs to be clever and personalized and needs to be time sensitive. There are times in my life when I might be interested in a new insurance contract or a new car, and there are times when it doesn't make sense at all. So being smart about that too is really important.

People talk about user experience and this is actually the first step in adoption. You go to a website, maybe a car manufacturer and maybe you're interested in it or maybe you just have 15 minutes to kill and want to look at the new Mercedes and you're just curious. [Y]ou [could] have a clever chatbot or something clever in the mobile app or in the website that creates the early relationship very high in the funnel that says 'Hey I don't want to bother you I saw you looked at this car. Do you know this fun fact about the car?' – or something that gives you extra information on a product or service and starts to build and engage but in a very human-like way and a friendly and hopefully fun way. Chatbots are a good way to do that [and] if you design them right – eg Alexa – [they] are a really good link between customers and your company.

Another example is we have a customer in the US – an insurance company called Liberty Mutual and it's a traditional insurance company. Many insurance companies have been around for a while so are pretty traditional and conservative. So Liberty Mutual are using our services, and they built a chatbot which in just a couple of exchanges lets you get a car insurance quote. We've all insured cars, and you go to the websites and you have to fill five pages of personal details before you even get maybe to a quote that you usually get by email anyway and that is inconvenient because you might be in the dealership and of course you're not going to do that. Whereas if you have a chatbot and you ask 'hey how much will it cost me to insure this 1968 Mustang?' and then just give a couple of details and get a decent quote. So this could be really personal and the chatbot might already know personal details about old cars and if you're a good driver etc, and it could be super personal and intuitive and it would create an additional business opportunity. So a lot of machine learning deals with perception – pictures, video, voice and text etc – and it actually learns to communicate with viewers. These systems behave in the most human-like way as possible – so they learn to communicate like humans and not the other way around.

Obviously, governments have a role to play with regard to regulation. GDPR is an important step for everybody, and it needs to expand and embrace and include everything AI related. Everything to do with customer data needs to be taken really seriously and it's good that GDPR is in place. All AWS services are compliant with GDPR since March, two months early. When you are trying to make things more personal and smarter etc there is a line you don't want to cross. It's OK if you bring value and extra information to customers and users, but they should always be in control of the last step, which is always conversion. Don't assume that they want to buy it – maybe they read the reviews and it's not good. You don't want it pushed on you; this may not even be legal. Common sense and decency goes a long way too. When you build something, imagine you're the customer. How would you react to that, how would you react to your kids getting this, or your 75-year-old mother facing this user experience? If the answer is 'not really', then why build it?

If we can use those technologies to make our world safer, cleaner, to give equal chances to everybody and education – I've got really high hopes of AI improving and democratizing education. It's fine if you're lucky to be at Harvard or MIT but maybe it's not an option if you live elsewhere in a less privileged place and if you can get access to the same education. All that stuff is important – I'm hoping that it will happen.

Technology is neutral and doesn't have feelings. There is no prejudice. There is nothing; it's just technology and what we make of it. We all have a fantastic opportunity to use this to improve the environment, education, healthcare, driving safety, security in general etc. And of course if we can make businesses more efficient and successful, I guess that is a step forward for everybody. That is what we should focus on, and of course there will be changes and some jobs will be transformed and some will be replaced. But this is the history of human evolution, so governments and the EU and so on have a role to play there to help with this transition. But we should really not say 'oh AI is scary, let's ignore it'; this is not going to help solve all of our current issues.

Next we take a look at Albert, the world's first AI marketing platform. Albert removes the complexities of modern marketing by performing many of the time-consuming, manual tasks that humans are unable to perform at the speed and scale required for efficient and effective consumer interactions (Albert, 2018). Recent news has announced:

> Albert Technologies is setting out to disrupt the digital marketing sphere with an AI platform that automatically generates campaigns for brands around the world. Albert announced that it has raised a fresh $18 million in funding from institutional investors that include Schroder Investment Management, Hargreave Hale and Old Mutual Global Investors. The round adds to an initial $42 million the company raised at its 2015 London IPO, back when it was known as Adgorithms.
>
> Among other enterprise vendors digging into AI: Amazon launched Alexa for Business, bringing its popular Alexa virtual assistant into the office to help solve business problems. IBM of course can't stop talking about Watson and credited AI (which it calls 'cognitive computing') with helping drive a recent turnaround after five straight years of consecutive quarterly revenue declines. Google is demonstrating Duplex, an assistant that can handle simple phone transactions well enough that a person speaking with it thinks they're speaking with a human. AI is a focus at Microsoft as well. And Cisco dropped $270 million on an AI firm, Accompany, and named that company's CEO, Amy Chang, as senior vice president in charge of Cisco's collaboration technology group.
>
> (Wagner, 2018)

In addition:

> Alibaba is investing huge sums in AI research and resources – and it is building tools to challenge Google and Amazon. Alibaba is already using AI and machine learning to optimize its supply chain, personalize recommendations and build products like Tmall Genie, a home device similar to the Amazon Echo. China's two other tech supergiants, Tencent and Baidu, are likewise pouring money into AI research. The government plans to build an AI industry worth around $150 billion by 2030 and has called on the country's researchers to dominate the field by then.
>
> (Knight, 2018)

Venture capital: pouring money into AI

We now turn our attention to the world of venture capital and hear from Davide Ferrara, Managing Partner, Macrina Investment Management.

He explains:

Marketing is a prime area for the application of AI. It has both lots of data available from which to 'feed' new AI constructs, as well as very compelling financials as to why one would wish to undertake such activity. Currently most AI in this space is being used to more accurately classify prospects and reactions to specific marketing campaigns. This is very much focused on generating higher 'conversion rates', a key metric for marketing. Over the next couple of years we should see this extend to AIs being able to also help chose what marketing approaches / models and routes to customers are best for each product and – ultimately – for each individual prospect. The level of granularity AI can bring in personalizing marketing messages will be a key frontier in the next two years.

Like all technology, AI is and will continue to first hit jobs that are well bounded, that is, which are repetitive or have well defined 'if… then…' type situations. Many of these jobs have already changed or been removed from the value chain by software and general automation. AI will be a further step in this, moving the focus to less linear situations, where multiple potential 'then…' are possible and a decision is required. It will also focus on any area where a lot of information needs to be considered or reviewed in making such decisions. The legal profession is a good case in point, where a lot of the case research and discovery of precedents etc is required in building a case. The problem here is that while lawyers will still be required, the training route to become one will be significantly disrupted as this is the work of Associates as they learn the trade. They will have to learn it in another way and there will also be less of them required (but not necessarily less lawyers required – thus the challenge). Another area is in medical services where we are already seeing AIs having better diagnostic capability than, for example, radiologists. Expect this to both continue and extend into other areas, such as diagnostics for most basic issues (anything a GP can handle), prescribing (in non-intensive care situations) etc. These are not your typical relatively low skill 'blue collar' type jobs, they are jobs that rely on many years of experience. Experience that AIs can... develop in a few hours... that is the real change when comparing the impact of AI to previous technologies.

The top of the field in most of this is Google's DeepMind. The $400m they paid for them, albeit originally criticized as 'hype' and a bad deal for Google will be seen by future history as the deal of the century! It really is. They are well ahead of anyone else. Further to what they are showing publicly (which is third or fourth generational AI), I am informed they are already working and alpha trialling sixth and seventh generation AIs. The relevance of this is that the generational scale for AI is not linear but more like an exponential curve. This means each generation is roughly 10 or more times as powerful as the previous... [which] makes for interesting math. There are many other worthwhile companies out there as well, although what Google has can be brought to bear on almost any economic area. A key point about all this is that the nature of AI means that there is significant first mover advantage involved. This is because once an AI is set to a task and given the ability to self-improve at it, it will inevitably do so and have a structural advantage of having started first. How does another AI catch up, unless it is 'smarter' at the point of starting? Self-improving or 'autonomous AIs' are the real way forward.

Change has already begun and is continuing. Although a lot of the commercial and industrial applications of AI are still not 'hitting' the end consumer directly, a lot of AI is and continues to be deployed by companies in all sorts of areas, from logistics, to order or claims processing, to cybersecurity etc. A lot of this takes place on the cloud or through cloud services, where part of the overall process is conducted by AIs designed specifically for that purpose. In the not too distant future we are likely to see more and more of these processes being completely undertaken by AIs, with talk already turning to the creation of human-less enterprises, where the entire organization sits on a computer and executes its value add[ed] in the economy through collection and issuance of instructions. From an end consumer perspective, we are already seeing some AI being deployed directly, whether called that or not. However, the reticence of companies to risk alienating or upsetting their client sets will make the introduction of AI to end consumers slightly slower as companies have more to lose if they get it wrong here. As with any new technology, there is the proving of it and the inevitable overcoming of resistance to change. Once it starts happening, however, it will accelerate quite quickly as companies can simply not afford to be left behind. Call centres, booking systems, personal helpers and – as more appliances become compatible – the Internet of Things will be the way end users will have the most direct contact with AI-based services. The next two years will see this extending, becoming the new normal within the five- to seven-year period. Driverless cars are a key bellwether to assess progress here.

Companies must very quickly come to understand that AI is not a fad, nor a threat, but an opportunity. They should approach AI like they do any other business proposition or opportunity. They need to first inform themselves, then identify cost-effective ways to adopt AI into what they are doing. It needs to remain driven by good business thinking and wise investment, as it is very easy to get caught up in the hype or make sloppy and ultimately expensive assumptions. Some of the problem with this is that AI is not always easy to understand. Secondly, it is also the case that many companies are run by people of age groups that are not those where the fastest appreciation of what AI can do is natural. This is a very real issue, especially as technological progress continues to accelerate. What was normal to one generation of managers is unlikely to be so to the next and so forth. The speed of change is forcing a considerable rethink of what it takes to be an effective manager, CEO or even Board member. Whereas experience and reputation was and remains important, the faster pace of technological change is increasingly requiring new skill sets, such as the ability to learn quickly or to understand advanced mathematical concepts. These are not the key traits for success in an industrial revolution or even service-based economic system or that current educational systems – even at MBA level – fully appreciate.

As to wider considerations, there are many. We discuss these a great deal within our Advisory Board (see www.macrina.co.uk for who I mean), as well as with leading thinkers on this. The ethical aspects are very interesting and important, and I have the benefit of also being able to discuss them with Prof Luciano Floridi at Oxford, who is regarded as the world's top authority on 'Digital Ethics' and the ethics of AI.

Our final contributor in this chapter is totally at ease in the world of venture capital and technology. Mike Fish is the Founder and CEO, BigData4Analytics. He explains:

AI is already transforming the way suppliers interact with customers (chatbots, Alexa etc). That's the visible part. And we've all heard about self-driving cars, but AI will also play an increasing role in 'autonomous everything' – self-optimizing marketing campaigns, product assortment and merchandising, pricing and market segmentation.

Activities with a high level of repetition are likely to be affected first (call centres, repetitive agency tasks). AI-powered marketing tools will boost productivity by doing more for the user. AI will also make high velocity or scenario-based tasks, such as crisis management, far easier. And AI's optimization capability should make it easier to carry insight through to automated actions, rather than dashboards that need people to interpret and then initiate actions.

We are very excited about US-based R4 Technologies, who have been a partner of ours for over two years. Their 'AI for the Enterprise' platform embodies their experience at Priceline and Booking.com, pioneers of the online airline ticketing industry. Their product already uses AI to, for example, make connecting to new data sources easy, to provide bottom-up auto-segmentation of customers and to carry insight through to automate and optimize actions. I believe that we will see material changes in the next 12–18 months.

Our analytics and AI work with leading companies suggests that success is now mainly determined less by the technology and more by 'Non-Technical Best Practice'. This ranges from having knowledgeable sponsorship at board level and the correct levels of ethics and governance ('the Digital Board'), through the challenging process of getting business and technical skills to work together to ensuring that employees affected by AI projects are properly informed of the impact on their roles.

Practical takeaways checklist: top 10 tips

1 There is currently a lot of hype surrounding AI in marketing, but the potential is huge, for example serving the customer with relevant adverts.

2 Real benefits can now be derived from AI because of the drop in price and the connectivity available.

3 Thanks to the availability of customer data and high connectivity, AI can now allow us to predict when a customer needs a particular product before they place an order.

4 Success with AI is partly achieved by technology but more importantly by strategic focus, for example knowledgeable sponsorship at board level and challenging the process of getting business and technical skills to work together.

5 Marketing professionals can turn to APIs and tools on a pay as you go basis, enabling them to stay small scale and experiment at almost zero cost.

6 Change has already begun with AI although much of it does not yet touch the end consumer directly, as it is focused on logistics, claims processing, cybersecurity etc.

7 You need to figure out a clear business problem that you want to solve, and if you cannot put it on paper in two sentences, it is not good enough.

8 Start with small problems and small questions. Don't try to solve every single problem with machine learning.

9 Don't be fooled by the scaremongers. Technology is neutral and doesn't have feelings. There is no prejudice. There is nothing; it's just technology and what we make of it.

10 We have a fantastic opportunity to use AI to improve the environment, education, healthcare, driving safety, security in general. That should be our focus.

References

Albert™ [accessed 23 July 2018] Artificial Intelligence Marketing, Albert™ [Online] https://albert.ai/

Forbes Middle East [accessed 9 July 2018] Dubai Goes Smarter as It Embraces Blockchain and AI, 15/04 [Online] www.forbesmiddleeast. com/en/dubai-goes-smarter-as-it-embraces-blockchain-and-ai/

GovInsider [accessed 9 July 2018] Exclusive: How AI is Powering Dubai's Pursuit of Happiness, 26/04 [Online] https://govinsider.asia/smart-gov/ ai-powering-dubais-pursuit-happiness/

Knight, W [accessed 23 July 2018] Inside the Chinese Lab That Plans to Rewire the World with AI. *MIT Technology Review*, 07/03 [Online] www.technologyreview.com/s/610219/inside-the-chinese- lab-that-plans-to-rewire-the-world-with-ai/

PwC [accessed 9 July 2018b] The Potential Impact of AI in the Middle East, 11/02 [Online] www.pwc.com/m1/en/publications/potential- impact-artificial-intelligence-middle-east.html

The Official Portal of the UAE Government: UAE Strategy for Artificial Intelligence [accessed 9 July 2018] [Online] https://government.ae/ en/about-the-uae/strategies-initiatives-and-awards/federal- governments-strategies-and-plans/uae-strategy-for-artificial-intelligence

Wagner, M [accessed 23 July 2018] Salesforce Sprays AI to Get the Stink off Customer Service, *Light Reading*, 7/11 [Online] www. lightreading.com/enterprise-cloud/machine-learning-and-ai/ salesforce-sprays-ai-to-get-the-stink-off-customer-service/d/d-id/744576

Wolverton, T [accessed 23 July 2018] A New Study Shows That Tech CEOs are Optimistic about the Future, Even If They Still Don't Understand Millennials, *Business Insider*, 22/07 [Online] http://uk.businessinsider.com/tech-ceos-kpmg-survey-optimism-fear- millennials-nationalism-cybersecurity-2018-7?r=US&IR=T/#tech-ceos- are-bullish-about-their-companies-growth-prospects-1

Framework for success

07

Democratization of AI

In this crucial chapter, we aim to consolidate the learnings from previous chapters and provide the marketing professional – and his/her fellow board members – with a plethora of invaluable insights and advice, combined into one pragmatic, implementable framework for success. Prepare to open your mind to ideas that will stretch your thinking, but simultaneously, you may find yourself reassured that many traditional strategic approaches to management and marketing are still applicable in the new world of AI. Our world is being reshaped by AI, and, now more than ever, human leadership is essential, in both marketing and wider disciplines. Finally, we have provided you with an invaluable scorecard against which you can track your progress.

Let's start by considering to whom such a framework is applicable. In other words, what size of company and which industry sectors will be able to exploit AI for marketing and wider business use more rapidly in the coming years? In seeking to answer this question, we must, once again, cast our net wide to ensure we provide an unbiased and extensive range of expert views on this very important topic.

Our first expert provides some reassuring views. Dr Peter R. Lewis is Senior Lecturer in Computer Science at Aston University, UK. He states:

> I believe there will be a democratization of AI to those companies
> without the resources of Facebook, Google and Amazon. An example
> of this is what we are doing through our Think Beyond Data project
> at Aston University, supporting SMEs to take advantage of the latest
> advances in AI to help their business to grow. Machine learning is giving

us image recognition, face recognition technologies. The larger players give us cloud-based services and APIs, which you can just plug into that. You can get the developers to integrate these kinds of features into your software. But there's not a lot of need at the moment to do the kind of bespoke implementations: it depends of course on what the business is trying to do. There are plenty of innovators around doing new things, but for most businesses, they can plug into the APIs that are available, or use standard open-source tools to get started with AI.

As we continue to unpack our unrivalled assembly of invaluable advice, we turn once again to industry analysts as a trusted voice. According to Mike J. Walker, who is Vice President, Technology Innovation and Enterprise Architecture Research at Gartner, the actions that marketers need to take with regards to AI implementation are many and varied. Walker states:

> The biggest thing is understanding what your company is going to look like over the next three to five years. You need to take the calculated risk in the areas that are most important because what is important today most likely won't be important tomorrow. Don't go beyond five years unless you are in defence or aerospace; they have to go 10 to 20 years forward. Understand what the 'to be' state of your organization is going to be.

The three essential questions we need to answer are:

1 What are our 'known knowns'? We know what the challenges are and we know how to deal with them.

2 The 'known unknowns'. We know the thing that will disrupt us but we don't know how to react to it. One example could be a bank dealing with blockchain. We don't know specifically how it is going to impact us, and we don't know how to use that technology to create new business opportunities and remain competitive in the marketplace.

3 'Unknown unknowns'. We don't know what's out there and we don't know what to do about it. This is a dangerous and scary place to be, as we cannot see the forest through the trees.

Walker continues:

> Organizational soul searching is vital to the marketing department.
> They can't do it alone; they need to partner with the business units;
> it's a collaborative effort. The worst thing you could do as a marketing
> professional is build an island, especially if the 'to be' state of your
> business, in other words, the traditional lines just doesn't exist anymore.
>
> It is essential to partner with the senior decision-makers. Don't just
> meet with the subject matter experts. They have opinions on everything
> but no authority. Talk to the people that have authority and would go
> to jail if things go wrong; their heads would roll if they missed out on a
> big opportunity. Figure out what you want to be when you grow up as
> a company. What action do you need to take? In terms of a framework
> for success, I recommend the following:
>
> 1 Figure out what your company looks like in three to five years.
> 2 Invest initially in the use of AI and machine learning in automating
>   the personalization of marketing and merchandising messages.
> 3 Choose use cases with the greatest possibility of automating away the
>   lowest-value transactions.
> 4 Pick analytics and information whose quality and credibility are
>   good and which have sufficient scope to fully address the problem.
>   Invest in efforts to verify and improve the quality of data for such
>   purposes with particular strength.

Understanding your data

Before we get into the steps you must take to produce a successful AI
agenda, you must first work out if your organization is prepared to
exploit it, notably, whether your data and infrastructure are in shape
to power such a complex tool. Professor Michael Luck, Dean of
Faculty, Natural and Mathematical Sciences, King's College London,
has some invaluable advice for marketers on this point:

> There is something crucial, which is about the education piece;
> understanding what the tools do and where they might be sensibly
> applied. Typically, they will be applied to data and to processes. Data is
> still relatively new; many companies are still finding out what data they

have or getting it into sensible shape to be exploited. Understanding what data you have and how you might use it is helpful. If you can work out what these techniques do, then you might be able to think early enough about how to get your data into the right shape to exploit it.

The start-ups and major suppliers are all doing different things. They are largely using particular kinds of tools but not exclusively so. The expertise is probably the same. For a simple bespoke off the shelf solution that looks like what many others are doing, then in some sense you don't need to design the particular thing in great detail. Where you want to be particularly innovative, something that not everyone else has done, so that you can't apply the standard toolkit, that's when you might want to think about what the more bespoke offering can do. So that's when you might want to think about what gives you an advantage over the competition in terms of doing something that others have not yet thought to do.

This need is echoed by Ludwig Konrad Bull, Scientific Director at DenninX. He explains:

What we do at DenninX is probably very similar to what a lot of companies or smaller companies are doing in AI right now. They are applying statistical tools and artificial intelligence tools to areas where there is just a lot of data. Law actually is an area where there is tons of data as well. There are millions of legal documents on the web. There are also a vast number of both legal publishers and law firms themselves. So, what we do is we focus on litigation and we help law firms and insurance companies and banks and governments analyse the data to make the right meaningful insights. Legal data as opposed to other areas of data is really complex and… it's not always clear and it's always extremely unstructured. It turns out that the profession that's really disliked by a lot of people for requiring a lot of paperwork actually has not left us very good records because things aren't structured when you're reading a judgement for example. So, one thing that differentiates the work that we do from other AI companies is that we actually have to use AI to structure the data first. So before we can even start using AI to derive insights from data, we also have to use AI to just structure the information.

Judgement and decision-making

Robbie Stamp is CEO of Bioss International, a global network of organization and people development consultancies. He explains:

As a company we are fundamentally interested in the nature of judgement and decision-making in complex environments, and in understanding the conditions that leadership creates around everybody in the organization being able to exercise their judgement effectively from the board to the front line. Conditions analytics are designed to give a board and the Executive team a line of sight into the conditions they are creating to allow everybody to whom the values and ethics, strategies and tactics, the reputation of the organization are entrusted, to be able to make effective judgements.

We look at three key metrics and this does have direct relevance to AI. Fundamentally, we look at coherence, so is the story that the organization tells about itself and the way it is perceived externally coherent? This organization knows who it is, why it is, what it is. The next part is judgement; is the organization collectively and effectively exercising its judgement wisely? Are people even allowed to exercise their judgement? The next piece is review and learning. If all organizations are social organisms made up sometimes of very large numbers of people, consuming resource, making decisions large and small, committing the organization to risk and opportunity, then how well adapted is that organism to its environment? Is it showing that it learns and consistently adapts?

One of the exciting things for us is we should get more and more predictive power in the data. One of the things that AI will do, when managed by good diverse data scientists (!), is look for and understand the difference between correlation and causation in patterns in vast oceans of data that are unmanageable for human beings. Greater complexity and systems fundamentally feed off information; if that is so, then the promise of AI, if we get it right, is this astonishing augmentation of our capacity to understand patterns in our world and genuinely make the world a better place, or maybe do what we can to minimize the destructive aspects of human nature and maximize the constructive.

Human beings have an overinflated sense of our ability to control outcomes and a terrible fear that we won't. So, when it comes to AI, what is different is that we have a new form of cognitive augmentation which goes beyond even the printing press in terms of the way in which it augments and potentially replaces a great deal of the work of the mind that humans have done for millennia.

Human judgement

An important question that is vital to consider when discussing the increasing control AI is having on many aspects, is when do we renounce human judgement? Will there be a time when healthcare and social care are overseen solely by an AI machine, or will the human judgement/touch be necessary alongside it despite its ever-growing competences? Talking on this topic, Stamp comments:

> Here's the protocol. I ask five key questions: Is the work the AI doing fundamentally advisory? Does it leave space for human judgement? It increases our capacity to understand, looks at patterns, but it is only an adviser. Next question – have you granted it authority over any human beings? Is anybody managed by an AI? With Deliveroo and Uber – the answer is unequivocally yes. An AI supervises you on a daily basis.
>
> Here is a thought experiment. If you push forward say 10 years and imagine a surgeon operating on the victim of a serious car accident, with multiple vital organ trauma. A sophisticated AI is monitoring vital signs. You get to a stage where it looks like the patient is going to bleed out. You have 120 seconds to make a life changing decision, but the AI and surgeon suggest different procedures – which do you follow? Who has the authority to make that decision in that pressured moment? Those that say 'back the AI' might argue that the AI isn't feeling the pain or exhaustion of another patient lost that morning. In addition, while the procedure has been going on it has been reading reviews of the latest medical papers from top hospitals worldwide and is recommending a brand-new procedure that has had fantastic results and can 'talk the surgeon through the procedure'. Maybe the hospital authorities have decided that no new procedure is ever carried out in

those kinds of circumstances and back the surgeon. If the advice of either the surgeon or the AI is prioritized and the patient's family sue, who is liable? Whose career is threatened? The hospital has to be clear who has the authority in a number of circumstances and what the consequences of exercising that authority might be.

Agency

The next question is how much agency have you granted the AI to commit money, resources, reputation, to expose an individual to risk, without a human being in the loop? For example, Netflix recommends films based on categories and films you have previously watched. But if you were to recommend *13 Reasons Why* (about teenage suicide) to a vulnerable teenager, who the algorithm had picked up through a wider search on social media, maybe even a simple AI recommendation engine is not so anodyne after all. Make it agency granted in the world's nano-trading markets or to autonomous weapons systems and the consequences are potentially global.

Abdication

Glancing back to the point on renouncing human judgement, we must be cautious of the boundaries of AI's capabilities and to what extent we grant it autonomy over crucial – and especially life threatening – roles. Stamp comments:

What do we abdicate to an AI and when? Take driverless cars; the idea that the AI can suddenly hand back control if they are suddenly 'unsure' about a driving 'event' and expect the driver to have both hands on the wheel and be fully aware after hours on the road not concentrating, well, that is nonsense. And it is a dangerous nonsense, too, to design a system on the assumption that this is what would happen. So, this is not a value judgement; there may be times when abdication is the right thing to do. The point I want to make is, be clear that is what you are doing. Don't pretend that you're not. It may be the right thing to do, to give the responsibility to the AI. But if you cross that boundary, think through the consequences. You can see that talking about abdication opens up another set of complex and fascinating issues, right the way through to the widest societal level. Just because we can automate cognitive work, should we? At what pace? Who gets to decide?

Accountability

On the topic of granting agency and autonomy to AI, it is no surprise that legal and ethical challenges arise. If we award such huge responsibility to these however remarkable machines, we must also endow them with liability and not be naive to their limitations. But how realistic is this concept? Can we simply hold an AI machine accountable if it were to be the cause of injury – or worse, a fatality? Stamp proposes:

Legal and philosophical implications go straight to the final question of accountability. AI cannot in any shape or form be accountable in the way in which human beings are accountable. It can be liable; there could absolutely be an insurance market growing which would say: if you were deploying your AI and it has the capacity for things to go wrong, you may take out insurance. This is not the same as accountability. Many people also mix up responsibility and accountability. In organizations made up of humans we know that one of the underlying tensions is that people are accountable for work for which they are not responsible. You may give me responsibility for doing something, but it could be you who is accountable to others (regulators, shareholders, government) if it goes wrong.

So think of it this way: algorithms are not separate from the ecosystem of judgement and decisions, accountabilities and authorities in organizations; they are an integral part and will only grow more embedded in the fabric of human institutions of all kinds. The Bioss AI protocol is an interesting way of analysing the moving parts of working relationships with non-human actors and consistently asking 'how's that working for us?' Who is 'us' in this context and who are we asking, and, by implication, who are we not asking?

Take advantage of what's out there

Next, we turn to the importance of transparency for humans in an AI era. While your organization may be offering a state of the art, enormously useful AI algorithm, without the customer's understanding of what it is and how it works, they are unlikely to trust the product or service. Without such explanation, we are asking customers to blindly trust systems that many do not understand. Therefore, if you cannot explain its reasoning, do not offer or deploy the intelligent system to begin with. Giving his interpretation on this, we turn now to Dr Peter R. Lewis, Senior Lecturer in Computer Science, Aston University, UK. Lewis is also Director of an initiative called Think Beyond Data, which is about supporting SMEs to take advantage of the latest technologies in AI, machine learning, data visualization and analytics, to help them to grow:

> In terms of a framework for success, my number one piece of advice would be to take advantage of what's out there. That includes the technology, but it also includes hiring the right people. Trust and transparency are also key factors. How are people going to trust you if they are buying a product and it's got a black box inside of it. You need to think about how you explain what the AI is doing.

Outward looking view

Robbee Minicola is Global Lead at Wunderman AI, a division of the global digital agency which help clients navigate this new technology. Minicola explains:

> My biggest message is get a strategy. Often you are too close to the strategy as a CMO. You can create a wireframe or thumbnail of what you want to do, but get someone outside your organization to help you build that. You need to have an outward looking view, not an inward one, when determining your strategy. You have to partner for this; CMOs and CIOs alone can't achieve this. You need SaaS partners, platform partners like Google Cloud, Microsoft Azure, AWS, IBM Watson. Being connected to one of these four platforms (at a

minimum) helps you see the future before it manifests; partnerships are super critical. If you are a medium-sized business the best thing to do is bootstrap yourself to Adobe and Salesforce.com. If you are a small company, just operate in conversational technology that's already available.

Unleash the potential of AI

We also spoke to Rob McCargow who is Director of AI at PwC UK. McCargow is an advisory board member of the UK's All-Party Parliamentary Group on AI:

> AI is emerging as the defining technology of our age, with many industries already utilizing AI in some form. It's now becoming critical to unleash the full potential of AI to transform your business model. AI is offering transformational possibilities for consumers, businesses and society as a whole. Almost every aspect of our daily lives has been digitized. Internet and mobile technologies have transformed the way that we live and work. A new wave of technology is coming through, and it centres on data. AI will utilize data to assist us with the many tasks that we currently do ourselves today and will be able to do things that we've never even conceived of before.

In terms of a framework for success for CMOs, McCargow recommends the following:

1 aligning with your strategic goals;

2 don't expect magic;

3 be clear about your partners;

4 open up to scrutiny;

5 demonstrate regulatory compliance;

6 look at the impact on the whole organizational structure.

Clearly one of the major global players in AI is Microsoft. Norm Judah, CTO, Microsoft Services, offers some reassuring news, especially for companies with more modest budgets. When asked in a

CNN interview about timeframes, Judah confirms that: 'You can build agile solutions in AI in weeks' (CNN tech, 2018).

Speaking to Mike J. Walker, Vice President, Technology Innovation and Enterprise Architecture Research at Gartner, his advice is clear:

It's less about their deep pockets. The key is their innovative culture, mindshare and risk-taking process. Which brings us to an age-old question of how to change the tyres when the car is still in motion. How do we take calculated risk? How does a leading organization properly scope and prioritize what is most important and attack those problems first? Sometimes it's not that easy. It will require your senior business partners to understand the importance of this technology's role in their business and make it a part of their daily routine to continuously challenge the status quo. You cannot simply create the ideas from the top down. You need to create a programme which involves employees; one which crowd sources ideas. Perhaps you could consider gamifying it and incentivizing staff to innovate... We are seeing more and more budget go towards CMOs, and it's being continuously distributed. We are now seeing CDOs taking a share of that pie as well; take for example General Electric who have implemented a CDO function.

Marketing ecosystems

Dr Elvira Bolat is a Senior Lecturer in Marketing, and Global Engagement Lead at Bournemouth University, UK. She explains:

In terms of a framework for success, companies need to consider the following: ecosystem thinking. To me, this is a way to move forward. We need to think about all key players within the industry; tech providers of hardware, software working closely with public institutions, research organizations etc. All of these representatives within an industry need to look into developing spanning capabilities. Spanning capabilities is about the ability to recognize resources and capabilities of all involved parties and then creating synergies that lead to strategic impact. Ecosystem thinking will enable industries to develop guidelines on aspects of ethics, sustainability and privacy. It is only this collective thinking that can take AI deployment onto the next level without the consumer fearing technology. Instead they need to be excited about the value it can and may generate.

Cultivating openness

Tania Peitzker, Chairwoman and Company Director of a French company called Bots as a Service (BaaS) SARL, comments:

> In terms of a framework for success, companies need to have clarity on terminology and understand realistically what AI technologies can and cannot do. It is amazing that many people, including technologists, think that a humanoid robot or avatar like the HUMANS androids in the TV series and other sci fi films are a reality that could be possible this year or next. We are at least 10 years away from that, purely because of the limitations in computing power.
>
> So once a company's management and staff understand the capabilities of any AI tech pragmatically, they should then do a checklist of what they want it to do for them and make sure the coders and technologists agree it can be delivered. That is the best way to guarantee return on investment when being an early adopter or bravely running greenfield pilot projects. Above all, companies should cultivate an openness and willingness to give these new technologies a chance – that is pay for their software services without haggling and license it appropriately – or these 'disruptive' new ventures will just be bought up by the US and Asian tech giants and the lack of diversity will kill off any genuine innovation for years to come.

One step at a time

In Chapter 5 we heard from Sherif Mityas, Chief Experience Officer at TGi Fridays. He shares three bits of advice for any marketeer considering how best to approach AI:

1 Start small – Pick a couple of use cases that you can really measure and show the ROI, because there are going to be a lot of doubters within an organization that hasn't done it. Focus on things that are measurable but that you can say, look at what it achieved.

2 Don't be the smartest person in the room – Get other people from the outside. Talk a lot to other people. There are lots of new innovative companies out there in this space, so bring a bunch of them in and learn. Understand what is going on and see what people are talking about.

3 Always bring it back to what you are trying to achieve – Whatever the metric is for you, try to tie it back to something that is key and core to the strategy, because then it gets people interested. It has to be integral to one of the key strategic pillars of the business so that it is meaningful when it comes out.

Julien Simon, Principal Technical Evangelist, AI and Machine Learning at Amazon Web Services (AWS) comments:

In terms of a framework for success, my number one piece of advice is always the same. What is the question you are trying to answer? Or what is the problem you are trying to solve? If you cannot put it in one sentence, then don't move any further. People still embark on machine learning projects and say 'we just need one because everyone seems to have one', and this is the worst thing. You need to figure out a clear business problem that you want to solve, and if you cannot put it on paper in two sentences, it is not good enough.

Number two is do you have the data to answer that question? The answer can be yes or no, and if you have the data then ok you can start working and looking at it. If you don't have the data then there are two options. You could start collecting it but that can be difficult. In the case of satellite images, you can go and buy satellite images. In the case of car insurance quotes, you probably have a few millions of those in your records so that's good, but for some companies it's not possible to get that data. If it's too costly or time consuming or whatever the reason is, then you should look at high level services like for example the one that AWS provides – image recognition services etc, and they are already trained on our own datasets and you can use them with zero data of your own.

The third problem or question is what is your skill level? How skilled is your company, and is it central to your business to build those skills?

This is a difficult one because if you really insist on building your own data and machine learning team, then these people are hard to hire and costly and it will take a while for that team to build.

What I see working really well is start with small problems and small questions. Don't go and try and solve every single problem in your universe with machine learning. That doesn't work; the Big Bang thing never works in general. It doesn't work for machine learning either – so pick small things. Don't try and create that super complex enterprise-wide project that is going to be scary, risky, hard to figure out that will take years.

Ten steps for AI in marketing success

My own three decades of experience in marketing, combined with a year of in-depth research in compiling this book – with unparalleled access to the world's leading experts – lead me to confidently recommend the following 10 steps for AI in marketing success:

1 Understand the dynamics of AI in your sector, now and in the future.

2 Devise your business strategy and then your marketing plan accordingly.

3 Start with small problems, focused on customer needs, and be prepared to fail.

4 Define your strategy for AI in marketing and set key metrics/key performance indicators (KPIs).

5 Prioritize technical AI competence: train, hire, partner or invest in the right solutions for the task at hand.

6 Reinvigorate your culture to embrace innovation and agility.

7 Collaborate across departments and reorganize where necessary.

8 Attract and retain the right staff and partners.

9 Invest in a continuous lifelong learning journey.

10 Adhere to – and play a role in – defining the ethics of AI in your industry/country.

Let's look at each of the 10 points in a bit more detail.

1 Understand the dynamics of AI in your sector, now and in the future

No problem or opportunity can be properly assessed in isolation. You need to research the current and potential future impact of AI in your industry sector, playing close attention to established competitors and potential disruptors. Disruptors will be those who can fulfil an existing customer need, or create a new one, innovatively, more cheaply or simply in a fashion that captures the imagination. AI may well be the key to that, but so too could other tech innovations, or simply new approaches to pricing; think Primark.

Armed with this knowledge, you must then decide whether you want to innovate, lead, keep up or just milk the market for the remaining time you have left.

2 Devise your business strategy and then your marketing plan accordingly

Again, this will be dictated by your ambition and your longer-term goals for the business. What is certain is that you need your marketing strategy to dovetail with your business plan. You need to consider how AI can support both.

3 Start with small problems, focused on customer needs, and be prepared to fail

The starting point for your AI marketing plan must be the needs of your customers/clients. If you don't obsess over them, your current – or future – competitors will. Also, remember that, given its early stage of development, working with AI will be a highly iterative and agile process and not a waterfall process.

4 Define your strategy for AI in marketing and set key metrics/KPIs

You need to start by defining success and setting clear KPIs. This will support you at the outset when making the business case for investing in AI marketing technology and also when justifying the results or feedback mechanism for the next phase.

Usage of AI in marketing will evolve. In time, the early adopters may well develop advantages over competitors. Important details are crucial too; for example, you need to identify the personality of the bot because it represents your brand. What emotion do you want to create in customers when they interact with it?

5 Prioritize technical AI competence: train, hire, partner or invest in the right solutions for the task at hand

In other chapters we have heard from a number of academics who are experts in the fields of AI and machine learning. It is important to heed their advice on the subject of technical competence. The best course of action will depend on the problem to be solved but will typically be one of the following: train, hire, partner or invest in the right solutions/tools.

6 Reinvigorate your culture to embrace innovation and agility

Build an agile operating model and a company culture that is focused on and adapts quickly to customer's changing needs.

Take inspiration from former Domino's CEO Patrick Doyle, who used technology to achieve a turnaround in the company's fortunes, thereby narrowing the gap with Pizza Hut, their major competitor.

7 Collaborate across departments and reorganize where necessary

AI adoption in marketing alone is not ideal. You need to form a cross-departmental strategy; one that optimizes data and resources for best effect, always keeping the customer at the centre.

8 Attract and retain the right staff and partners

Communication with all stakeholders is a central role for all market-ers, which is more reason for marketing to collaborate with other teams such as HR to help attract and retain the right staff and partners. Given the dominance of AI in today's business headlines, business people will increasingly be asking probing questions about their organization's readiness for this new world.

9 Invest in a continuous lifelong learning journey

To thrive in an era of unpredictability, you need teams who appreciate the need to continuously push themselves out of their comfort zone. However, changes in behaviour and culture can be hard to absorb, which is why the marketing team is so crucial in communicating the importance of this agility internally and to the wider supply chain and to future staff.

10 Adhere to – and play a role in – defining the ethics of AI in your industry/country

Set out your own ethics and principles of fairness. Also adhere to the policies in place within your own country and industry sector. Where they don't exist, or are merely embryonic, don't hesitate to play your role in helping to define them. Consider important issues of bias in consequential services, and always keep top of mind the values and rights of the citizens of your country and of the world.

No strategy is not a strategy – remember that not having an AI strategy is not an advisable plan if you want to succeed in this new world order.

AI in marketing scorecard

Armed with this invaluable advice from leading global experts, the marketing professional is now exceptionally well placed to create a new strategic marketing plan that incorporates AI and needs to be aligned with the organization's wider business plan. To assist, we have prepared this AI in marketing scorecard (Figure 7.1), against which you can track your progress. There are 10 focus areas, each containing 5 key points, allowing for a potential total score of 50.

Figure 7.1   AI in marketing scorecard

1. AI MINDSET	2. C-SUITE SUPPORT	3. BUSINESS CASE	4. EXPERIMENT	5. COLLABOR-ATION
✓ Vision ✓ Openness ✓ Ability to change ✓ Flexible ✓ Realistic	✓ Comfortable ✓ Eager ✓ Aligned ✓ Active/ partner with decision markers ✓ Driving forward	✓ Solves customer need ✓ Strategic KPIs in place ✓ Iterative approach ✓ Processes ready ✓ Tracking competitors/ disruptors	✓ Know which tools can help ✓ Proof of concept ✓ Prepared to fail ✓ Processes documented ✓ Cohesive data for deep insights	✓ Inter-departmental ✓ Humans and machine ✓ Work with academia ✓ Links to supply chain and partners ✓ Long-term vision
1 point for each	1 point for each	1 point for each	1 point for each	1 point for each

6. AI TALENT	7. CULTURE	8. INNOVATION	9. WIDER IMPACT	10. ROADMAP
✓ Continuous learning ✓ Reskilling plan ✓ Executive talent ✓ Dedicated resources in place ✓ Funding available	✓ Interdepart-mental ✓ Outward looking ✓ Fairness ✓ Long term ✓ Recognize the 'what's in it for me?' factor for staff	✓ Agile ✓ Encourage innovation ✓ Open ✓ Planning for disruption ✓ Planning for transform-ation	✓ Understand ethics ✓ Work with industry trade body ✓ Input to frameworks ✓ Responsible/ vigilant ✓ Compliance	✓ Strategic plan in place ✓ Aware of funding ✓ Success criteria in place ✓ Ready to execute AI ✓ Authority to proceed
1 point for each	1 point for each	1 point for each	1 point for each	1 point for each

HOW YOU SCORED/50?	0–20 – Traditional	20–35 – Transitional	35–50 – Transformational
	Currently operating more traditionally; a novice in AI but at least it's on your agenda. It's time to research your industry, identify the available tools, be clear of the customer need and begin to create your AI in marketing plan.	A promising start; AI is on the cards, but you are missing many opportunities to make a major impact. Look closely at your score and analyse where the gaps are and where you can focus your efforts.	You are exploiting the benefits that AI can offer in many aspects of your marketing. In order to make a transformational impact on your business, review your score and analyse where the gaps are. Keep the customer at the centre; take a long-term view and consider the wider ethical impacts of AI.

Visit **www.aiinmarketing.com** to complete your scorecard.

These 10 focus areas are as follows:

1 AI mindset;

2 C-suite support;

3 business case;

4 experiment;

5 collaboration;

6 AI talent;

7 culture;

8 innovation;

9 wider impact;

10 roadmap.

Your final score will place you into one of three categories:

A score of 0–20 – Traditional

Currently operating more traditionally; a novice in AI but at least it's on your agenda. It's time to research your industry, identify the available tools, be clear of the customer need and begin to create your AI in marketing plan.

A score of 20–35 – Transitional

A promising start; AI is on the cards but you are missing many opportunities to make a major impact. Look closely at your score and analyse where the gaps are and where you can focus your efforts.

A score of 35–50 – Transformational

You are exploiting the benefits that AI can offer in many aspects of your marketing. In order to make a transformational impact on your business, review your score and analyse where the gaps are. Keep the customer at the centre; take a long-term view and consider the wider ethical impacts of AI.

Visit www.aiinmarketing.com/scorecard to complete the test online.

Remember that it is an iterative process and, rest assured that despite the hype, if you do score low, you are not alone.

Reference

CNN tech [accessed 9 July 2018] Microsoft: You Can Build Agile Solutions in AI in Weeks [Online] http://money.cnn.com/video/technology/2018/06/13/microsoft-ai-solutions.cnnmoney/index.html

The new marketing paradigm

08

Reinventing the role of marketing, ethics and transparency

The CMO's rise to fame

In this chapter we zoom our lens into those at the coalface of marketing and PR, seeking to establish exactly what the new marketing paradigm is in this new world of PR. We turn to the US, France and the UK and hear from industry bodies, agencies and brands. We also reveal the findings of a study into views about AI in China and the UK; this study was conducted using an AI tool which is disrupting the market research sector.

We start by talking to Robbee Minicola, Global Lead at Wunderman AI, a division of the global digital agency which helps clients navigate this new technology. Minicola explains:

> Many companies feel that their own proprietary data is in disarray. They have a preconceived notion that because their pantry [of data] isn't in order that they can't do anything. Many companies feel paralysed because they have some ridiculous notion that their data is not ready, and I think that is largely because CIOs traditionally were in this everlasting job of boiling the ocean to clean up that pantry.
>
> When the concept of big data came in some 10 years ago, the volume and the variety of data was plonked somewhere in a heaped mess, possibly on AWS (infrastructure as a service) and somebody just

slammed the door shut and prayed to God that nobody needed to access it. Smart CMOs started to say: 'Hey I need to get more insights but the pantry is such a mess that getting insights feels impossible'. The first insight the CMO got was the data he/she controlled in their own business unit. Companies like Salesforce.com became popular because they focused on the CMO (not the CIO), and they helped the CMO get sophistication around what they could learn from their data.

Getting closer to customers

The CMO's rise to fame in data and predictive analytics didn't really come from an innate desire to hang out and party with the CIO. What happened was that CMOs had a need to achieve automation and ROI on their activities. They were thinking: 'I have to get closer to our customers and I have to have better capabilities and rules on how I engage with audiences and measure my ROI and my expenditure'. In doing so, the CMO went out and sought partnerships that had data in it [sic] and a degree of analytics so that they could make better decisions. These activities heralded the CMO as a sophisticated player in the organization related to analytics and predictive analytics. There was a disruption of sorts when Adobe and Salesforce[.com] were working directly with the CMO to drive marketing and customer outcomes which, at the same time, helped them understand the value of platforms and SaaS. This was the turning point for CMOs.

Democratizing data to secure customers' insights

When business intelligence came in, it added a level of sophistication to historical data and democratized data so that everyone in the CMO team or even in any other division of the company could have insights in the palm of their hand to make their own informed decisions. These tools (Tableau, Power BI, etc) allowed the CMO to pull data from products like Salesforce[.com] and Adobe and get insights in real time about how their business was performing. Business intelligence tools represented the tipping point for CMOs, and they wanted to do more with their data, beyond measuring what happened in the past. As they started to make conscious decisions about the data they collected and where it goes, they were ready to now use data to predict.

When I see clients, the first thing I ask is: 'Tell me how you are using business intelligence'. That was the biggest indicator to me as to whether or not the marketing organization valued data. If they had a level of sophistication with BI, then you pretty much knew that they are hungry and ready for the next step. If they want to use AI in their business yet have never used BI, then there is a learning curve we will need to go through. It's a crawl, walk, run process. *Crawling* is amassing insights from the data you have (BI). *Walking* is when you discern the difference between historical insights from structured data and predictive outcomes from unstructured data (ML). *Running* is when you have both working in tandem across both structured and unstructured data. It is in the running phase that you are ready to start using fully autonomous machine learning algorithms (AI).

A good starting point for AI for any company, even those without sophisticated data analytics, is *conversational technology*. The idea of conversational technology is converting every one- and two-way *communication* with your customers into two-way *conversations*. The effect of this is building a voice strategy that heightens engagement and helps your customer realize their needs in real time and in a non-linear fashion. Think about it, we design websites and mobile phone applications in a linear fashion, but people don't think linearly. A conversation, even with a machine, is better in that it allows a person to start wherever they wish to and glean what they need to know that is particular to them. Imagine hearing what customers want to know about first, then retrospectively adapting your one-way communication to respond to those. It will revolutionize the way you talk to customers.

Many people confuse a voice strategy with simply building a 'skill' on Alexa or Google Assistant. That is not a voice strategy. A proper voice strategy is when you convert and create your own two-way conversations on your platform, then add skills on third-party devices to augment what you have built between you and your customers directly. This is important as the third-party platforms are not suitable for PII data, nor are they HIPAA or GDPR compliant. Finally, if you use third-party voice platforms, then all of your conversational data is with the third party – not yours. We propose a centralized database of all conversations (spoken with a voice assistant and texted with an intelligent chat system). In this way, customers get a seamless experience across devices. Where a company has more than one brand, you can connect conversations at the back end and learn quickly where a customer is using more than one of your brands.

With more than 400 million people speaking to Siri, 500 million speaking to a Google Assistant, 150 million people speaking to Cortana, more than 20 per cent of all search occurring through voice – we know that the world of typing and reading is transitioning to speaking and listening. Thanks to machine learning and cognitive services (AI), we can create customized conversational solutions for brands on Microsoft Azure, AWS, IBM Watson and Google Cloud.

How will AI impact marketing?

The top three areas where AI will impact marketing are media purchasing, media metrics – which is what a marketer spends money on when they are trying to get effectiveness from the media real estate. From a machine learning perspective and a deep learning perspective, that is number one. Group M have services that have artificial intelligence in it [sic] that help understand and optimize media buying. The second one of the three for marketers is around customer journeys from prospect to acquisition, to on-boarding, to retention to win back. This is the role of business intelligence and machine learning; not yet deep learning but I think it will go there in a matter of time. In most companies, the only two-way conversation that they have is in customer care or in a retail environment or both. The capability of having conversations with customers from text right through to text-to-text, right through to visual to voice-to-voice, it's huge. That automation is also a beautiful and elegant data collection mode that gives you primal understanding of how customers want to communicate with you in a non-linear way.

Your early adopters are already adept at using data insights as it is part of their core business, not just marketing. Financial services, banking, credit cards, insurance companies; these companies are already adept at collecting data and have large data pantries and mine this data for the success of their business. These are the ones who are the early adopters of this because they already have their kitchen in order and they can just make new dishes with the data in their pantry. The next group that are following are the ones who have high platform usage ie they have a lot of sophistication through use of Salesforce.com or Adobe.

In terms of the rest of the world, the tipping point will probably be two years. It's going to get to the point where you can't compete if you don't have your ducks in a row. In my view CMOs today are more sophisticated than many agencies. There is a new round of CMOs. It's no longer about taking clients out for a boozy lunch. It is about being able to sit across the table from them and have an intelligent conversation with them and their team about how data and insights can drive predictive measures for them to be successful in their business and derive proven ROI.

The sophisticated CMO

If you can't sit at the table and talk at that level then you are done. I think the agency leaders of the future are people that are going to come out of predictive analytics, people that have a strong data background. Just as CMOs are becoming sophisticated, I think agency leaders will no longer be account leaders that go 'oh yeah I'll go find out for you'. It's the person sitting at the table going 'listen, let me tell you' with data at the coalface. They are either going to be platform experts or analytic experts, or they are going to be creatives with elegant problem-solving skills.

I believe that GDPR represents an opportunity, although it is in Europe; I think that all the platforms AWS, Google, Amazon and IBM Watson are all ready for GDPR here in the USA too. I think it's an opportunity because when you get the right legislation and parameters in play and in the best interests of the consumer, and when you get the right level [of] permissions associated with that instead of it being them and us, their data and our company, it can be the 'we', the customer and us. Because what you're doing is optimizing the data but keeping the customer in control. The whole idea of optimizing my ads on a website or as I browse through, surreptitiously looking at me and serving me what you think I want; instead you give me control, showing me what I want to see. It starts to drive a trust equation between myself and the brands that I associate with. Then the brand becomes a service to me instead of an annoyance, so I think that not only in an acquisition mode but also a retention mode.

The concept of 'always on' has been around a few years. We have had the mobile phone and we had the internet and therefore 24/7 access. We thought that 24/7 access meant always on. I think where we're going is not 'always on' but 'always serving'. When brands say they 'are we always on?', today that means you have to go to them. That's the wrong direction. They need to be 'always serving', meaning they are predicting your needs and supporting you in your life endeavours with the services that they provide. CMOs are trying to get to 'always serving', and I think if they do that then the generations to come and as our high school and middle school kids grow up, this always serving approach will create a beautiful balance between the consumer and the organization. A hybrid of something we have never had before, which is an exchange of bi-directional loyalty.

Much talk is that AI will cause people to lose their job. I think if someone came to me and said, I'm 16 years old and I don't know what it is I want to do, could you give me some guidance. I would say, go with your penchant for being creative or technical/analytical. If you have neither and you want to work with your hands, be a tradesman because we are always going to need plumbers and electricians. They are the backbone of our society. The middle jobs will be at risk. In terms of ethics, the number one rule is transparency and permission. Be transparent about what you are doing and ask permission before you do it. We have to think very judiciously about how we use people's data and the impact it has on their lives. They should be liberated by it, not victims of it.

Next, we hear from Francois-Xavier Pierrel, who is Corporate Director Data, CRM and Social at Groupe Renault. He explains:

To make it clear, automotive at this stage is probably not the main user of artificial intelligence. It is not that we don't like it. It is not that we don't have an interest in it. But if you look at the way the sector has operated, it is the same way for the past 50 to 60 years. This is one of the last industries which hadn't been hurt by a deep disruption.

The main disruptor today is Tesla. Actually, the only thing they do is put electric engines in cars. This is a great achievement, and I'm really supportive of it, but at this stage Renault is still the number one company selling electric cars in the world, which proves that disruption is not there yet. Tesla is still struggling to produce volume.

Deep learning can really advance AI with regards to autonomous driving. This will probably come on the road within the next 10 years. Some markets will be much faster, but for the moment the area where we could use AI the most is in R&D. We don't have pure application of it; we do have some examples such as autonomous braking coming. We will really take advantage of AI when we have autonomous driving with a lot of calculation where you have to interpret a lot of strong and small signals along the way.

For sales and marketing, I think at this stage we are going to be positively stuck on machine learning for quite some time because we are not a digital native ecosystem. We are not booking.com; we are not an airline or Facebook, so we need to first revamp and build up our data the right way. The key step for us will be around security and having capacities to anticipate an issue and tell the customer and the driver for example that their tyres are getting flat, and that they should go to the next dealership to get them checked. This is AI helping to improve security through machine learning.

If you want to leverage AI to improve marketing in this sector, you will see an emergence of chatbots, instant messaging, decision trees etc to answer specific problems. Let's take an example: if you are driving your car and get a flat tyre on the highway. You'll try to find your 'flat tyre kit' but then you are frustrated because you can't find it, you will open your tray and try to find it but it is not there for some reason. It could be under the passenger seat or some other area of the car. But as you are in an emergency situation, you want the answer right now so you can imagine having a bot to which you will ask the question: 'where is the key to change my tyre?' Or you might have a video screenshot showing you how to do it but also giving you the option to call directly for assistance to get it fixed on the highway. So this is where we believe having artificial intelligence even at the easiest levels will help us bring value without specifically looking at monetization.

This is about information on the customer and the ability to fix these irritation points you mentioned and give them a very personalized service. The fact that the AI or data points through say an API is enabling a human to offer that level of assistance is actually very powerful. Whatever we do, customers or users are central. You can leverage chatbots or Messenger for a million reasons, but if you get away from bringing value then you are not getting the usage you wish and so you get more frustration.

Reskilling for AI

AI is doing more than just improving the customer experience and advancing data analytics tools; it is also reshaping marketing teams, as we know it, including how we hire in marketing. According to Business2Community, 'leveraging martech to reach your goals faster is a given, but what you might not have considered is how implementing such technology – like advanced automation and AI – will naturally shift the hiring profile of your marketing staff members'. Here are three ways AI will change the way you hire your marketing team, according to a recent Business2Community study:

1 **Hiring critical thinkers for entry-level positions** – Today, everything from writing headline copy to serving highly personalized ads can be done with AI, so entry-level marketers will need to have more critical and analytical minds than required in the past. Entry-level jobs will involve synthesizing information and applying context to ensure that AI outputs align with the proper intent.

2 **Asking creative leaders to be more data-driven** – While creative minds will keep a company fresh and cutting-edge, marketing teams of the future will be more data and consumer driven.

3 **Recruiting more marketing generalists** – As AI-driven marketing tactics continue to proliferate, more repeatable tasks will be offloaded to machines. This will accelerate scaling and consolidate existing marketing positions, and, over time, one marketing generalist may be able to handle the work of several specialists with the assistance of AI-driven technology.

Customer centric value

The Business2Community study continues:

What we want to deliver is customer-centric value and it is not always about buying stuff but just getting the right answer at the right moment and making the customer feel that she is being taken care of by automized solutions like chatbots. It's about evolving and having the capacity to say this is an issue and my chatbot interaction needs to [be] coming to an end so I can redirect this to a real person.

Renault is specifically a company which was built on innovation. Initially it was innovation about the engines and the shape of the cars. But innovation is in the DNA of the company. There is an appetite for new stuff and for innovation and disruption which is extremely strong, so we don't have to convince our bosses that AI is key. The question in such a big organization is one related to consistency in direction and governance and understanding the value you want to deliver through AI.

If you start delivering AI, you need to have responsibilities and you need to be extremely careful about what you are going to do with it. Where are you going to draw a line that you are never going to cross? This is about making sure that our customers – the end user – understands that we collect data and that we use technology to improve service and to become as customer-centric as possible.

Great power brings great responsibility

If you have great power, you have great responsibility, and autonomous driving is about this, and collecting data is about this. You need to be sure that you don't cross the line in the wrong way. What we are referring to then is transparency and accountability.

My advice to companies getting started with AI is to put your feet in your customers' shoes. What is the value you bring them? You must be agile and flexible. Marketing needs to be able to control their destiny, keeping your hands on the wheel and making sure you find the right co-pilot.

R&D is divided into many business units. The guys working on autonomous driving, the guys working on data lakes; plus we have our own sales and marketing for the moment and we have data scientists and analysts. We're also exploring bigger and better platforms like IBM Watson and Microsoft Solutions, ensuring that we leverage some platforms but not too many or it will be too complex for us to manage.

Even at the lightest level of instant messaging we've seen a lot of value. For automotive it will help in the way in terms of creating autonomy, more security, more safety and probably more services.

Views from the public relations industry bodies

Francis Ingham is Director General of the UK's Public Relations and Communications Association (PRCA) and Chief Executive of The International Communications Consultancy Organisation (ICCO). ICCO is the voice of public relations consultancies around the world. The ICCO membership comprises national trade associations representing 55 countries across the globe: from Europe, Africa, Asia, the Middle East, the Americas and Australasia. Collectively, these associations represent over 2,500 PR firms. Ingham states:

> I'd like to say that AI will impact PR positively, but it's really too early to say. My assumption is that the industry will ultimately embrace the new business opportunities delivered by the rise of AI. But as PR is only just beginning to contemplate the issue, it's hard to predict. The industry is gearing up at different paces, but I'd say the distinction isn't really between sectors. It's between size. The big companies owned by holding groups are starting to invest and gear up. When you go to a small agency, it's quite naturally business as usual. The obvious aspects of work, which are likely to be impacted first, will be monitoring and reporting. Quite frankly, these are the elements where our industry expends its time least profitably. So if we can save resource here and invest it more profitably elsewhere, then we can profit from AI. There are many AI related companies and tools on the market to assist both in-house and agency PR teams. In my opinion, 2025 would seem a reasonable guess for change to really begin. In terms of a framework for

success, my advice would be to follow what the big guys are doing. Take advantage of their investment by learning from their mistakes. And by big guys I don't necessarily mean from within our industry.

At the BledCom Conference in the summer of 2018, I saw an academic paper presented on AI. Its basic conclusion was that developers were entirely ignoring the ethical challenge that it throws up. So associations like the PRCA need to get involved here. The same principles of honesty, truth and regard for the public good are as relevant here as in any other parts of the industry.

Next, we hear from Stephen Waddington, former Chartered Institute of Public Relations (CIPR) President, and Partner at Ketchum, who, in January 2018, set up a panel on behalf of the CIPR to explore the impact of artificial intelligence (#AIinPR) on marketing and public relations. Waddington explains:

> The market for tools in PR is exploding. A crowdsourced exercise has characterized more than 120 tools. AI has become a catch-all term to describe technology that engages with people or displays human characteristics. It is unhelpful and is contributing to hype and uncertainty around the topic. The CIPR #AIinPR panel defines AI as a sophisticated application of technology whereby a machine demonstrates human cognitive functions such as learning, analysis and problem-solving.
>
> Each tool has been labelled by function and AI sophistication using a five-point scale (Figure 8.1).

The last two levels on the scale represent what the panel deems to be AI:

- simplification – technology that simplifies a PR process, or provides a tactical service;
- listening and monitoring – media and social media listening and monitoring tools;
- automation – automation of tactical tasks;
- AI for structured data – machine intelligence applied to structured data;
- AI for unstructured data – machine intelligence applied to unstructured data.

CHARACTERIZATION OF
TOOLS IN PUBLIC RELATIONS

Simplification of tasks
• Databases
• Wire service

Social listening and monitoring
• Brandwatch
• Talkwalker
• Mention

Automation of tasks
• IFFFT
• Open data formats

AI for structured data
• Google Analytics
• Newswhip
• Traackr

AI for unstructured data
• IQ Bot
• Quid

#AIinPR

Future proofing for AI

Waddington advises:

I would urge anyone to take a proactive approach to technology within their organization. Here are some ideas for introducing a culture of innovation:

1 Learning and development – Explore the changes that technology is driving in media and PR. There's a growing body of knowledge related to AI and the professions. I try and spend at least 90 minutes a day reading, and deconstructing information via my blog.
2 Investigate the third-party tool market – The vendor community is keen to sell into the PR market. As a start point investigate tools that could help deliver your existing work smarter or more efficiently. Listen to vendor pitches and ask to trial tools for yourself.
3 Make and break, test and learn – The current wave of innovation is creating a huge variety of new channels for public engagement. These include messenger bots, voice marketing and image recognition. Appoint people within your organization to investigate different forms of technology, and the opportunity to create new services.

Tech, AI and tools vs skills in PR

The narrative around the impact of AI on professional jobs is typically polarized between denial and techno-panic. A second piece of work by the CIPR has attempted to understand how AI is impacting PR practice and its workforce. A study led by Jean Valin, Principal of Valin Strategic Communications, on behalf of the #AIinPR panel, found that right now 12 per cent of PR skills are being assisted or impacted by AI. Machines are already undertaking tasks such as data analysis, horizon scanning and data management, performed by practitioners starting out in their career. The CIPR project shows that given the pace of development of software and machine learning, that number is expected to rise to 38 per cent in five years. By 2023 AI will impact areas of PR such as stakeholder mapping, risk analysis, auditing and behavioural analysis (Figures 8.2 and 8.3).

Figure 8.2   AI in PR today, 2018

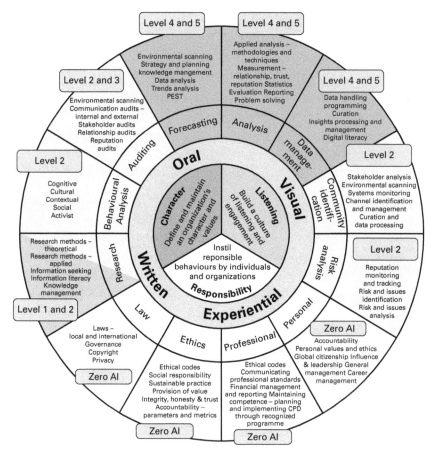

SOURCE CIPR (Chartered Institute of Public Relations). Original image courtesy of the Global Alliance for Public Relations and Communication Management

Jean Valin explains:

> The business case for tasks that could be replaced by AI is clear. If it makes business sense to replace repetitive, predictable or scriptable interactions with a bot, it will happen. Voicebots or chatbots will dominate the marketing process, especially client interaction.

Figure 8.3 AI in PR in 5 years

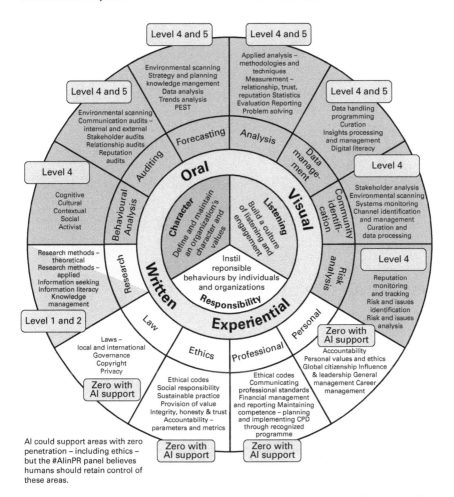

CIPR CHARTERED INSTITUTE OF PUBLIC RELATIONS

#AIinPR in 5 years

Tech and AI Scale
Level 1: Simplification
Level 2: Monitoring
Level 3: Automation
Level 4: Machine intelligence structured
Level 5: Machine intelligence unstructured

SOURCE CIPR (Chartered Institute of Public Relations). Original image courtesy of the Global Alliance for Public Relations and Communication Management

Public relations has more breadth of activity, which as our report says, involves tasks that are less likely to be replaced by AI. Ethics, law, humour, empathy and professional conduct could be assisted by AI, but humans must remain responsible for the final decision in these areas.

Companies who are not exploring how AI and automation can help with analytics, forecasting and report generation will miss the boat. The power of AI is that it can do what humans did in days and weeks in hours and minutes. There will be ebb and flow and lots of consolidation with AI tools and products as with any nascent technology.

Lessening the burden of minutia

Peter Loibl, President and Chief Strategy Officer, CONCURED, comments:

> I hear rumblings from content marketers that AI technology will eventually usurp their value and roles within their respective organizations. But I strongly believe that AI will lessen the burden of a marketer's day-to-day minutia, providing more time and focus to doing what they do best: harnessing their creativity and telling great stories.

Disrupting the market research sector with AI

Chris Kahler, Co-founder and CEO at Qriously, comments:

> AI and machine learning techniques are at the heart of Qriously's new research methodology, called Programmatic Sampling, which works by replacing ads with surveys in smartphone apps in real time. Traditionally, research is conducted with panels composed of paid respondents who are allocated into representative quotas to reflect a certain population being studied. The problem with this method is that there is an inherent bias in respondents who are being financially compensated, it's expensive (respondents need to be recruited and compensated) and slow. Additionally, recruiting panellists in certain countries can be difficult and expensive – for instance, in India, the standard method of conducting market research is still using human interviewers with clipboards in the street.

Programmatic Sampling leverages the fact that many people have smartphones with ad-supported apps in them; many countries particularly in Africa and South East Asia have 'leapfrogged' the PC era and gone directly to smartphones. In Egypt, for instance, smartphone penetration is comparable to Western Europe. Qriously uses AI and machine learning techniques to make sense of the huge amounts of unstructured and inconsistent data that is passed in advertising exchanges to make predictive models of a studied population. Much like driverless cars use computer vision to distinguish a pedestrian from a lamppost, Qriously uses machine learning to predict whether or not a survey response is from a bot or a middle-aged woman, in real time, to produce a stream of representative responses. In terms of scale, the amount of data processed to make these real-time decisions is staggering: 1.8 billion people generate over 100,000 'requests' or pings from their smartphones every second, which have to be evaluated by hundreds of concurrently running machine learning models to assess key demographics and truthfulness.

At Qriously, we have developed a way of modelling the responses of users to questions, in particular demographic characteristics. To summarize, for any user we can generate several hundred features which we can use as the input to models which return the probability that the user has that demographic profile eg the probability they are an adult, the probability they are female. We use our survey answers as labelled data when generating these models, but the system allows us to evaluate the models against any user we see in the bid-stream, whether or not they have interacted with us before. We can use either the individual feature values as a pre-filter to bidding, or use a full model as a way of excluding those users who are very probably not those people we are interested in. Most commonly we have used a model which excludes users very likely to be under 18 years old or have filtered out people we think are under 13 years old.

The biggest disruptive force we can apply is speed and scale. Qriously surveys can be conducted instantaneously in over 150 countries on the planet; we can have thousands of respondents answering our surveys quite literally within minutes. While panel providers can sometimes imitate this scale for large projects, their speed naturally falls off once most panellists have been contacted.

Qriously doesn't have this problem, as we can reach so many more people. For example, one client asked us to survey car owners in a long-running European study; we ended up surveying over 5 per cent of the adult population of Norway(!). No panel provider could hope to compete with that kind of range. In another example, a music streaming brand asked us to survey parents of teenagers in the UK. We ended up interviewing over 200,000 adults in the space of just a month or two. Data quality is another area where we outperform most competitors. Qriously has successfully predicted dozens of political elections – including ones where the vast majority of pollsters were wrong (Brexit, Trump).

Market research in China and the UK using AI

In order to generate some unique market data for this book on attitudes to AI in the UK and China, we decided to put Qriously to the test. Using this disruptive AI tool, we carried out a survey that was distributed across the UK and China to people aged from 13 to more than 65, with an equal gender representation within the sample. A key theme revealed in the survey was the universal consensus of ethics and regulations surrounding AI, with 74 per cent of respondents from China and 69 per cent of respondents from the UK, agreeing that this was an important issue to be addressed (Figure 8.4).

However, interestingly, there were some significant differences in openness and trust towards AI between the UK and China. Less than 6 per cent of respondents from China reported that they would feel 'very uncomfortable' having robots in the workplace, compared to 25 per cent of UK respondents. Similarly, nearly 29 per cent of respondents from China reported they would feel 'quite comfortable' with having robots in the home, whereas the same percentage of UK respondents stated they would feel 'very uncomfortable'. In addition, 35 per cent of respondents from China, as opposed to 13 per cent from the UK, stated that they 'somewhat agree' to the statement 'I completely trust chatbots'.

Figure 8.4   Qriously AI market research survey

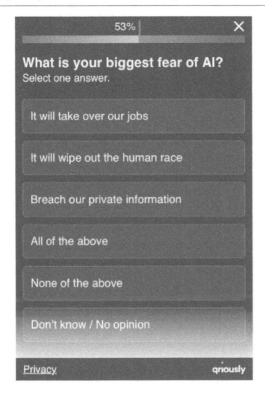

Despite these stark differences in accepting AI into our lives, respondents from both countries considered themselves to have a very similar understanding of AI, with 44 per cent of UK and 47 per cent of Chinese respondents reporting that they have a basic understanding. Therefore, the contrast between the two countries may be a product of other factors, such as how much AI has already pervaded our lives. Despite only 10 per cent more respondents from China compared to the UK reporting that they 'somewhat agree' that 'AI has already impacted our lives', China already has more robots than anywhere else, and their obsession and openness to accept them is thought to be linked to the ageing population (Abacus, 2018). Partly due to the one-child policy, it is predicted that one out of four people in China will be over 65 by 2050 (CNN, 2016). This means that China's workforce is reducing and, to stay competitive, they must turn to automation.

Practical takeaways checklist: top 10 tips

1 The early adopters are already adept at using data insights as it is part of their core business. Financial services, banking, credit cards, insurance companies; these companies are already adept at collecting data. Using AI they can now mine this data for the success of their business.

2 Marketing agency leaders of the future will probably come from a predictive analytics/strong data background.

3 AI will give us information on the customer and the ability to fix these irritation points with a very personalized service.

4 The PR industry is gearing up at different paces. The big companies owned by holding groups are starting to invest and gear up. But when you go to many small agencies, it's often still business as usual.

5 Companies who are not exploring how AI can help with analytics, forecasting and report generation will miss the boat.

6 The power of AI is that it can do in hours and minutes what humans did in days and weeks.

7 Once you start delivering AI, you need to have responsibilities and you need to be extremely careful about what you are going to do with it.

8 It's essential that customers/end users understand that you are collecting data and that you are using technology to improve service.

9 AI can enable you to become highly customer centric.

10 It's really important to take a proactive approach to technology within your organization.

References

Abacus [accessed 9 July 2018] Why are Robots So Popular in China? 8/3 [Online] www.abacusnews.com/future-tech/why-are-robots-so-popular-china/article/2136418

CNN [accessed 9 July 2018] How Quickly Can China Come Back from One-Child Policy? 13/10 [Online] https://edition.cnn.com/2016/10/13/health/china-one-child-policy-population-growth/index.html

The future of marketing has arrived 09

AI's wider impact on education, policy and politics

Scratching the surface

As we have illustrated in the earlier chapters, the world is in the midst of the fourth industrial revolution, and we are only scratching the surface of the moral, ethical and legal concerns posed to society and individuals by the increased use of robotics and AI. In this, our final chapter, the marketing professional must reflect on these learnings and consider a number of key questions: will robots and AI do more harm than good? Can we teach robots ethics? And is the landscape of AI 'boundless'? For this we turn once again to world leading academics, brands, tech disruptors and policy makers.

In a world of change and uncertainly, one thing is clear: AI and robots will change the world as we know it. Whether this change is for the good or bad has not yet been concluded with consensus. While AI and robotics are believed by many to be pivotal in achieving economic progress, many protagonists, and those on the sidelines, are vocal with regards to our moral imperative to define regulatory standards of ethics, accountability and transparency. So let's now investigate these growing concerns, while also acknowledging the profits to society that this explosion of intelligence is contributing.

Farewell to dirty, dull and dangerous?

Dr Philippa Malmgren, founder of H Robotics, is a leading activist and advocate for the role that robots will have on our future economy, especially their impact on the 'dull, the dirty and the dangerous jobs' that will ideally be replaced by robots in the foreseeable future. In the BBC's *The Big Question* debate on whether AI and robots will do more harm than good, Dr Malmgren insinuates that it offers a positive opportunity for humans to upgrade their skill set more continually, to adapt and learn to keep up with the vacant jobs. She states: 'the economy, even without robotics, demands that we all adapt and change, that is a permanent feature of the world economy. If you add robotics into the picture, it arguably speeds that process up' (BBC *The Big Question*, 2018).

Increased productivity

Besides the palpable contributions that AI and robotics can contribute to our workforce, another question that has come to the surface is whether it has the capacity to redefine our job culture. It is the common and perhaps understandable judgement that the younger generation is typically more equipped than the elderly to fill specific job roles due to their physical proficiencies, despite the latter age group perhaps having greater knowledge and expertise in that industry. Dr Malmgren argues, however, that the robot revolution has the power to redefine the 'elderly', as automation can provide an immense opportunity for those who did not have the physical capability to re-enter the workforce, to take on newly available job roles. An example would be the handling and controlling of robotics and artificial intelligent machines, in an industry that does not require any extreme level of physicality. This opens up a new pool of jobs that can be utilized by all types of individuals. Ultimately, what we will see is a vast injection into the economy not only through the opening up of the job market by an increase in these available jobs but also due to the possibility for productivity to increase as a result of human beings remaining in work for much longer and doing a variety of different things that were not possible before.

It is indisputable that tech companies across the globe have made big advances in building artificially intelligent software that can make home and work life easier. Not everyone, however, sees the future in which AI is going to continue to play a major role in the culture and economy as a positive.

Redundancy of human beings

If you see the replacement of the above jobs as a negative, then it is likely that you are on the reverse side of the good vs bad argument, holding the view that AI and robots will do more harm to our society than good. Ian Goldin, Professor of Globalisation and Development at Oxford University, estimates that 35 to 40 per cent of UK jobs are currently vulnerable to replacement by robots. In order to prevent damage to society, Goldin advocates the requirement for new jobs to be created to prevent redundancy of human beings. It is not a question of who can do a task faster or more efficiently, but it is now a question of what we can do that is unique that can prevent us from being replaced. In order to survive we must create our own USP (BBC *The Big Question*, 2018).

Rising inequality

As we have come to see, artificially intelligent systems and robots easily replace repetitive, monotonous and routine job roles. But what about on a wider scale? Does it have the capacity to stringently raise inequality and impact the wealth gap like many sceptics are suggesting? After all, we don't live in an egalitarian society where we all have access to the same resources – so will the creation of robotics lead to the rich getting even more powerful? Kathleen Richardson, Professor of Ethics and Culture of Robots and AI at De Montfort University, UK, believes the answer is yes:

[w]e live in a hierarchy with power differentials – if you automate, you take away ordinary peoples' capacity to get jobs in the world. Companies are trying to digitalize all the different forms of manufacture, because once they can do that they can use algorithms and they don't have to employ human beings. They aren't going to redistribute their resources, they aren't philanthropic and they will keep it for themselves – [eventually] leading to more inequality.

(BBC *The Big Question*, 2018)

Algocracy

Charles Randell, Chairman of the Financial Conduct Authority, has made headlines as he warns of the danger of a new 'Algocracy' as new technology threatens to harm consumers of financial services.

Randell suggested that the concurrent rise of big data, AI and machine learning, along with behavioural science insights, could require a new regulatory framework. New technologies 'call into question the adequacy of the traditional liberal approach to the relationship between financial services firms and their customers', he said in his first public speech since taking up the role in London. He continued:

And regulation is central because it will help define whether AI and big data liberate customers or disenfranchise them.

Giant tech firms such as Google and Facebook have built up vast datasets and the ability to mine them in highly profitable ways but have also faced a string of scandals about how they use their newfound power. Financial firms, which the FCA regulates, while further behind, have started to rely on algorithms rather than human judgement in many decisions in ways which may prove harmful.

Society in general and policy makers in particular need to think about how to mitigate the risk that an algocracy exacerbates social exclusion and worsens access to financial services in the way that it identifies the most profitable or the most risky customers.

(Jolly, 2018)

Ethical matters

If we are to truly delve into the concerns surrounding AI and robots playing a greater role in our lives, it is important to recognize the current framework of society that we live in. Recent concerns submerged in the deluge of AI and robot headlines include the belief that some robots are 'racist', arguably stemming from a current dark skin MIT employee who is not recognized by a robot project and therefore must wear a white mask to communicate with it. Moreover, in US courtrooms, judges are increasingly using algorithms (instead of cash bails) to predict which criminal defendants will break bail and either flee or commit another crime, despite having shown bias against black prisoners and prisoners from a postcode in poor parts of the country. But can a robot truly be labelled 'racist'? Do these harmful traits of the robot not lie with who is building the robots? And should the blame not be on the human beings who possess these implicit biases, or with society as a whole that is comprised of biased laws and stipulations? After all, it is not the modification of racism or sexism but the codification of these traits – the robots are merely a reflection of the biases and inequalities we have as a result of society. In order to prevent these harmful traits from transcending, we must start by ensuring that we minimize bias problems from the get-go by designing AI systems and codifying robots with data that reflects a broader range of human experiences and interests. Removing all biases from robots is an enormous task and will take time. We must be aware that the harmful traits, which may lead to rising inequality in the long run and which are being exposed in certain examples of robotics, are not the fault of the artificial machines or robots but the invisible hand creating them. Our AI and robotics are only as good as the humans who create them.

What about 'its' rights?

One of the most confounding elements that we are grappling with in relation to AI and robots in the present day is the legal and ethical implication. It does not seem to have gone unnoticed with industry leader Google, who is currently facing tough demands for an ethical framework on the use of AI. In an attempt to respond to these queries, Google is creating a set of ethical guidelines for its employees to follow in line with its use of the technology. But will there come a stage in our technologically complex and challenging world where sophisticated cases of AI machines and robots are deemed to be a 'person'? If so, when should they be granted human-equivalent rights, freedoms and protections? Once, or if, this occurs, an answer will be far greater within reach, and when that time comes, it is unlikely that experts come to a full agreement. After all, rights are not just about consciousness or presence of mind but also capacity of suffering. We don't like to be hurt or injured, and so we have rights to protect us in society because we are susceptible to danger in day-to-day life. Are these robots taking on these sometimes dangerous roles also subject to harm? Are they subject to torment and harm by humans? And if so, should they be protected by the law?

When does it become dangerous?

Advancements in AI and automation in general are both exciting and terrifying, and with the arrival of any prodigy, cynics will abound. Given the flood of headlines on the fears that machines and AI are creating, it is quite understandable that people begin to worry whether these machines will surpass human capability. Will they start thinking for themselves and stand up to humankind? But at present, there is no need to fear AI and automation's impact. Of course it would be naive to believe that AI systems of such hyperintelligence couldn't pose serious problems in terms of ethical, moral and economic implications. But the fear of a hostile takeover by robots in this present day is far-fetched and should remain with Hollywood producers. That is not to say, however, that we mustn't regulate how they are used. It is important to maintain control over these super sophisticated structures which are becoming more capable by the day. Part of our responsibility for those at the forefront of production and manufacturing is to ensure that they do not monopolize and that they are not manipulated by others, especially as there is scope for intentional harm. Again, if this were to occur, the answer to how we manage this will be traced back to the accountability of individuals surrounding these systems. But for now, we can regard AI and robotics as a miracle tool.

According to Peter McBurney, Professor, Informatics Department at King's College London:

> We should be genuinely worried. There are all sorts of things that could go wrong and that may have already gone wrong. No programmer is ever completely confident about programs. We know that programs can have bugs, and in particular when you have complex systems where there are multiple programs written by different teams that are interacting with each other in ways that no one predicted. There is potential for another high level of bugs.
>
> Every technology over the last 200 years has resulted in some people losing jobs, but it creates new jobs for other people. There will be new marketing roles such as those with deeper insights from AI combined with domain and modelling expertise. These people will be able to understand human motivation and intentions. We are 50 years away from having machines that can do that.

Resilience

Trevor Hardy is Chief Executive Officer at The Future Laboratory. He believes that people and businesses are more resilient than we give them credit for:

> There could be short-term moments of uncertainty and may be job displacement due to AI. In two to three years many automated jobs may start to disappear. But over the longer term, say a 10-year period, there will be an increase in jobs we cannot yet imagine. AI poses a number of ethical questions, such as 'what are we striving for?' Western economies are on a path towards growth at all costs; innovation at all costs; and accumulation of wealth at all costs. There may be a point at which there will be a moral reckoning and that GDP is not the thing we should be striving for and accumulation of wealth is not necessarily going to bring happiness. There is a balance.

Are humans ready for help by AI?

But are we ready for AI to assist us? Lewis Richards is Head of 21st Century Human Practice at Leading Edge Forum (LEF), a global research and thought leadership programme dedicated to helping clients reimagine their organizations and leadership for such a tech-driven future. He explains:

What we are seeing at the moment is an explosion of what we call narrow AIs that are appearing in business. The Holy Grail is artificial general intelligence, but we're not near that yet. So, what we are seeing is the application of narrow AI, which applies to business processes with varying levels of success. Are humans ready to use the AI to help them do their jobs? This is part of the challenge we are at now with all narrow AIs. The tools can do the tasks they are designed to do, but the actual impact it is having is going to vary immensely based on non-AI factors and very much on how digital is your HR department, and how integrated is your IT department. You also can't talk about AI without talking about big data and analytics – it's an end point of a combination of things. You can't talk about it without an understanding of IoT and 5G networks.

AIs will never get worse, and we will get closer to artificial general intelligence, so you can't afford to bury your head in the sand and think well this won't affect me. It is important to understand and take responsibility for yourselves to understand how it will impact individuals. Regulation and government will always be woefully behind the speed of science, and this is the problem. Most people are sheep and muppets and don't know how to use technology. We don't really have the skill set to be expert at it, only a very small minority of people do, so regulation has to try and balance that out. It's an incredibly difficult concept.

I don't think AI will substantially reduce jobs in the next two years, mainly because I don't think IT organizations and leaders in the business are geared up enough to re-factor their businesses in that way. The question is, could you build a brand new business that predominantly uses AI to do PR with significantly less people? Well probably yes. But traditional businesses may have thousands of people who do that and have the capacity in their organizations to do that. So I can't imagine anyone being really successful at doing that in the next two years. To do so, you would have to have such a strong ambitious C-suite team in place.

There is no right horse to back in AI at the moment. There are all the big players who have their own ecosystems; some more open than others. But I think what you are going to see is an incremental usage of AI technologies around the vision, algorithmic employment, which will have an impact and improve the efficiency of the business. But coming in and doing what humans are doing and replacing them? No chance; not in the next two years.

Trust

What is becoming apparent is that we need to understand when we can trust intelligent systems, or the extent to which we can, and when we shouldn't. Dr Peter R. Lewis is Senior Lecturer in Computer Science at Aston University, UK. He is also Director of an initiative called Think Beyond Data, which is about supporting SMEs to take advantage of the latest technologies in AI, machine learning, data visualization and analytics, to help them to grow. He explains:

We are putting machines into more and more positions of making decisions. You can't guarantee the particular intelligent system that is engaging in lifelong machine learning in a complex environment that is poorly understood. The machine needs to be able to have some level of awareness of its trustworthiness. It needs to be able to turn around and say, I have the confidence in my ability to do these tasks in this context.

The professional ethics would be a guiding set of principles for people who do understand what they're doing and what they're trying to do. So, for example, if you've got the machine, which is capable of essentially impersonating a human to do a task, it should have been required to identify itself as the machine. We need to think about who takes responsibility for what intelligent systems are doing in the world. Consider the self-driving cars and their crashes. So whose responsibility is that? It's not about blame, but it's about saying who's responsible for actually making sure that doesn't happen or trying to fix it when it does. I think this is about people stepping up and taking responsibility for what they're building, and we have a role in universities to do that.

So I think that's something that a business should take seriously in terms of how it engages with those questions. And my prediction is that people will start to expect and demand more. It might well be an ethical framework to manage what we're expected to do in that space. Going right back to the sixties, people were saying that computers were going to do all the work and no one would have a job anymore. That clearly didn't happen. So we need to decide what we want them to be; is it about more computers that can automate everything for us? It's interesting how quickly technology changes. Ten to 15 years ago there was a massive spike in jobs for web developers for example. That declined because making a website is quite easy now. So the point is industries and work evolve.

Actually one of the things we would like to see is machines slowing down a bit so people can observe what they're doing and check the decision rather than just everything having to be faster and more automated. Maybe that isn't what we always wanted after all?

AI that diffuses

All around the world, academics and policy makers are grappling with these issues. Danielle George is Professor of RF Engineering, Vice Dean Teaching and Learning at the Faculty of Science and Engineering at the University of Manchester, UK. She adds her views to this fascinating debate as follows:

It is important to remember that new ideas like AI create value really slowly as they diffuse, so it doesn't really follow Gartner's hype cycle at all. Sometimes there is a frustration or a deviation from what is true and what people perceive and that starts when the hype hits its peak. The actual value of that new thing is still very low; this is what sometimes creates the backlash. It's important for AI and robotics that we do have a lot of innovation. We need this innovation culture with all ages but especially the next generation of engineers, scientists and technologists. We need to manage innovation as a process, and I don't think we do that at the moment. It's not enough to just come up with ideas. We need time and resources; we need to select the best ones and make sure that we execute these. Otherwise we have too many things coming out. It floods the media for a while and then it goes away again. If we just get the best ideas to spread, then maybe the idea that terminators will take our jobs will disappear. We also need to get women more involved in building robotics because automation is becoming very white male.

Generally, for robotics and AI there needs to be more regulation. There is a huge ethical angle to this, which we – the human race – are just waking up to. Take for example the fact that a robot has more rights than Saudi Arabian women. That is so wrong on so many levels. That was a marketing gig done very well. But it points to the fact that there is a huge ethical framework to be set up. From a tech company perspective, there needs to be something done.

The Frightful Five – the undisputed rulers Google, Apple, Amazon, Facebook and Microsoft. These companies will dominate for a very long time and that is because they have built all of these enormous technologies and they are central to everything we do. If you think about what those five do, they are in healthcare (eg IBM Watson's oncology) and finance because of their AI engines. Some of them are building driverless cars eg Google, drones, VR, robots. They can branch out and do that because of their platforms, the users and all of the data plus of course the money; it puts AI very much within their grasp. They form this gilded mesh which blankets our entire economy. We can't get away from them, no matter what we do. It's disappointing that five companies dominate and will do for some time. Nobody is ahead of them; they are ahead of the game. So when they do something we don't expect, like going into finance, no one can act until it's too late.

We need international law to deal with AI; it can't change on a national basis. It's an international opportunity and challenge which cannot be addressed parochially. These big tech companies have a duty of care to make sure they are involved in the doing for good. I am very positive about AI. There will certainly be job losses, but new jobs will be created as well. I am optimistic about the future of jobs. I see intelligent machines and AI going to places where I wouldn't want to send humans eg disaster zones, war zones, nuclear decommissioning. There will of course be unemployment uncertainty, but I think AI and robotics can do far more good which outweighs the negative aspects. Everyone needs to get on board with the fact that they, and by that I mean AI, deep learning, smart machines and robotics, are here whether or not you want them or not, and it is defining our era. Markets, financial investors, can ill afford to ignore its impact. It will impact every industry I can think of.

If you took the human side out of it, that sociable piece, if you just think about the progression from teenagers now and the way they interact with tech and how different they are socially. If that projection carries on, even if it is just linear, I could see a future when our high street and banks look very different, a lot more interactive online and using technology very differently to the way we use it now. But there's a generation thing. We are never going to change the 60- and 80-year-old and we shouldn't want to. It should be available if they want to. They have grown up with a very different culture and a different social standard. I'm convinced that my 3-year-old won't have a driving licence in the way I have one. It will be different within 15 years.

A lot of people are playing at it in-house now. People don't know where else to turn. It can be good but only if everyone shares where they are failing. In the corporate world, that doesn't happen. Smaller companies are more agile and often do it more successfully because of their approach and their size. They have a different mindset which gives them a different agility. They both have different strengths. The smaller tech companies are starting from the clever PhDs; these start-ups often get bought by the bigger companies. You need a regulatory body because there are these clever people in these research institutes, universities, and it's a fantastic puzzle which needs solving. They are clever and want to be challenged technically. But it might not be the right thing to do.

From the tech point of view, I think there are enough people to go around. They are very in demand right now, but there are plenty of them in the pipeline. It's not the tech side that we have the problem with, it's the other sides such as looking at the landscape of where AI could go. That's a very different mindset to someone who is just interested in the deep learning and the maths. We need more of those with the business minds too. You need the application; you will always have these very clever people who will drive the technology forward for technology's sake. We also need the end users and the applications to be there.

AI is already a member of the team, working together with humans across all industries already. Personally I don't see the humanoid robot walking around in the way we do taking off hugely, certainly not in the West. In the East, they have a very different relationship with robots, and they have a lot more humanoid robots. Take Japan as an example, in care homes. We don't seem to have that relationship with them. In the West it seems to be much more of an industrial relationship with robots. I think it's cultural and based on our roots with the industrial revolutions. We see them more as slaves; they are doing something we want them to do. I do see a lot more AI and robotics but just not in the clumsy humanoid form in many ways which we don't necessarily need to replicate.

Another leading academic is Professor Michael Luck, Dean of Faculty, Natural and Mathematical Sciences at King's College London. He states:

Because AI is, or certainly has been quite a niche area, we don't have enough people who understand it or think about it adequately. There will be people who are able to use the tools, who can plug them together and use the APIs and do the things that they want to do with them. They will be rebuilding different versions of the same solutions. The worst thing that will happen is that they will be applying techniques to the wrong kinds of problems and not getting particularly good results. The danger is that people might then say AI can only do certain things; or it's not very good at something else, because they are conflating a particular technique associated with a particular problem to AI more generally. So the skills question is about ensuring we have enough people who understand the breadth of the different kinds of technique, tools, solutions and algorithms available, to be able to work out which kind of problem merits which kind of solution; when to use TensorFlow and when not to; when to use some of the deep learning or something fundamentally different. When to put the two things together in some really helpful way. We have a real shortage of people who have that kind of skill. A typical science undergraduate may have between one and three modules out of say 25 on their degree that are focused on AI. There are more degree programmes, at master's level for example, that have more breadth and depth. All of those people are really needed.

Off the shelf AI in less than 20 years

On the one hand this is just computing, but not just corporate computing but computing where there is some consideration for the algorithms and techniques being used. It's not just about databases.

To some extent, some of it will find its way into off the shelf tools like TensorFlow. And as it becomes more embedded into off the shelf software, it will be much easier for people who do not have the in-depth knowledge. In 20 years' time we won't be talking about AI, we'll just be talking about computing. Things that were once AI, stop being AI. At some point in time, Windows was called Windows NT; it was new technology – object oriented. That is the basis of most software systems today. But we don't bother calling it new technology anymore. That will happen to AI and that means that people will either be familiar with it or they will be using it without having to know too much because it will be available off the shelf. That will be fine for the standard things. But we are trying to do new things; trying to be innovative. We're doing much more than we ever could before; we're finding new problems and new solutions, which is why we need that expertise.

The other part of the story is that you can't ignore the fact that it is just computing. So, the basic skills that you need to be able to write programs and understand the fundamentals of computing are also necessary to be able to understand the fundamentals of AI. It's the same thing. So, you need the foundation. What we teach in schools is therefore an interesting question. You still need to be able to do the programming in order to think about the AI aspects. You have to build on the foundations. It's about making sure we have more visibility of the different AI techniques and get people out into the workplace who understand not just basic computing but also what they might be able to do with it in these applications and areas of technology. We introduced a data science master's programme last year at Kings; we've just had the second intake. We've had to close applications because we simply can't cope with the numbers. That's an indication of the demand from people who think there is a job for them and a demand from employers.

Regulation and responsibility

With regard to regulation and responsibility, Luck believes that there are two different parts:

One part is about how we in our human societies manage systems where there is not a human taking responsibility. We need to think about the ethical, legal implications. We need to understand where responsibility lies. We need to understand who is legally responsible; is it the designer; is it the programmer, is it the user; or is it the company? At this point in time we simply don't have the answers to these important questions. It's legal, it's ethical, it's social. There are questions here about what kind of world do we want to live in. There has be some regulation which is about how basic systems operate in our environment; in our society and in our world. There's another part which is about what are referred to as killer robots and to what extent we are prepared to allow decisions to be made by a machine when it comes to lethal force. There is a campaign against killer robots, and it's crucial that we do put in place controls, like there have been for landmines. Some of these technologies have the potential to be used for very bad purposes. It's not about the AI; it's about the fact that one can do many bad things with them.

Reputation and trust

How will these systems work with us in our society? Not regulation but trust and reputation. There are many tools and techniques which we humans have learned to use, not because they provide us with guarantees of what will happen but because they give us some degree of assurance. We interact with some people and not others because we trust some people. We shop in some places and not others. We have trust in some organizations. How do you develop that trust? How do we develop reputation? We also have norms and things that guide us in our interactions with others that may not be as hard as legal constraints but bring some negative consequence in the real world or even in our minds, which cause us to behave in certain ways. We are getting to a point where we will need to use these techniques to bring that same degree of assurance to computational systems and to AI. There is a range of things that we can do. We can look at the computational analogue of these human inspired constraints that we apply and we can apply those, for example applying that to the behaviour of the robot or the AI. We can verify and prove that they will not do some bad things.

Complying with regulation

Just as humans can today, the robot can be taught to behave differently in different countries depending on their laws, norms and customs. If they are to be useful, they will need to be adaptable. If they are to be useful, they will need to be able to learn from their environment. If they are to be useful, they will need to understand that they are moving to a different environment and in advance, anticipate how they might need to moderate their behaviour to fit in with that different society or organization. I see machines taking on more of the informal techniques that humans use to be able to function effectively in environments that are dynamic, uncertain, full of humans and have all sorts of difficulties for us as humans.

AI is not distinct except when it is in the power it can bring to bear. Does North Korea not do things that others have agreed not to do? There does need to be regulation, but the question is whether people will comply with that regulation the same in relation to nuclear weapons, chemical warfare, landmines. It is not different. What is different is the sheer capability of some of these things to be able to take us to a whole new level of engagement. That's where it gets challenging. It gets scary where you don't need a human in the loop; that's when regulation is crucial.

Vigilance

We are a very long way off from anything approaching the scary visions people talk of. I think we are 50 years away. AI can do bad things and cause major disruption. Think of computer viruses; add AI to that and you could cause huge difficulty. We are still looking at situations where there is initially a human responsible eg the person who sets off the virus. I'm not concerned about some of the warnings that some have argued about for some time. I do think that even if we're not going to get autonomous robots walking around policing things or doing bad things, any technology brings with it the potential for causing some difficulty. We've seen that for hundreds of years; it's not a few things, but we do need to be vigilant and careful because the pace is so quick and the capability is so high. Policy makers are starting to become aware of it. I have a concern around the recent hype around AI because I don't know that it is creating a bubble of expectation that can't be sustained. However, there is something really good about this which has raised the debate.

Scrutiny

Work is being done across the world in different guises and different forums to discuss different aspects of AI. There are some issues arising as a result of autonomous vehicles, as a result of a few deaths. They are significant in making sure people understand what the limits of the technology are and what we need to be careful about. The truth is that in many cases the numbers of deaths is smaller than it would be with human drivers, but that's not the point. The point is that we are getting the right level of scrutiny of these things. This hype is good in raising awareness of some of these challenges. People are trying to raise scrutiny for genuine reasons. There is a desire to make sure we don't walk blindly into something we don't fully understand. And there is a legitimate debate about the timelines for getting to greater capabilities. It's good and important to have the debate and think about the potential negative consequences. And it is good to pay attention and ask the question of what do we want of these new technologies.

Are these negative predictions right?

It's right to have this debate and this visibility. We need to do so calmly. We are not in doomsday scenarios. We need to take sensible actions. I don't see the future of the human race doomed in any way. We just need to think carefully about what we are doing. I think we have been doing that over the past couple of years, and we have seen a very significant change in the debate, which is important.

Referring to general AI, Luck states:

We are a long way off. We have today the ability to do some things really well eg voice recognition and image recognition. We can even work out what's in many pictures, but we still get it wrong a lot and we still have an incredibly long way to go. I believe that the last couple of years will cause much more investment in AI and that we will therefore make progress perhaps faster than we have been. But I still believe that we have some difficult problems to solve. I am optimistic. I think the pace will be sensible and will make a difference to the progress we can make in the coming years. I don't have too many concerns about us all being jobless and put on the scrap heap.

A shift as opposed to a new business world

Every revolution that we have had so far where people have talked of vast numbers of under-employed people has not resulted in those effects. I think there will be a shift; I think people will have to do different things. There may even be a period where there is under-employment as we go through that change. It may be more of a focus on service rather than traditionally industrial manufacturing roles etc. I do think it's about the shift and the change, not about a fundamentally new place to be. Will there be some difficulties because people are living longer? That's not about changes to technology, that's about changes we've been having anyway. What might happen is that the use of these technologies might speed that up a bit. A lot of effort will need to go into education, training and re-training to account for the new reality. Yes there will be some people who will find that they are unable to change and adapt, and things will be difficult for them. We do need to pay attention to that. But I think it's about freeing us to do more and different[ly]; to do things that we did not have the time or the capacity to do previously. Or freeing us to have more meaningful lives in our general day to day.

Inflated expectation and continuous investment

It's so hard to predict timeframes because things could develop in different ways. The recent few years and the recent successes could mean that we now move really quickly with huge amounts of investment in AI and we get so much more progress than we anticipated before. It could also mean that people have massive inflated expectations about what this will deliver; and it won't deliver that in the near future so we get what happened 30 years ago. So we get disillusionment and we get a lack of investment after a little while. Then they might stop paying attention to AI and move on to something else. That negativity may lead to slower pace.

Steven Struhl is CEO of Converge Analytic. He explains:

AI might well continue to displace some workers, and that would gain many headlines. However, AI should continue to provide more benefits quietly in the background, as we see improvements in, and wider adoption of, a host of analytical methods that address specific problems. Although these methods are not splashy, and often are hard to explain, they will help us see more deeply and address strategic and tactical problems accurately where we traditionally were left to guesswork.

Exploratory phase

A leading voice in AI, certainly in the UK, is Innovate UK, the UK's innovation agency and part of the UK Research and Innovation. Innovate UK believes there is more of an exploratory push happening right now. Two things are holding it back. First, skill sets in the UK and globally. By this we mean the availability of data scientists and people with the experience of the application of machine learning models. We are now seeing tools that abstract away from the nitty gritty. For example, Amazon, Microsoft and TensorFlow all make it easier for people to try to apply AI. There are still hurdles, but they are somewhat overcome. This needs further development to make it easier still for those who don't have the expertise. Second, there is a lack of real available datasets. The key is bringing a dataset together with another dataset. Machines can start to see useful correlations and have real predictive power. But different skills are needed. You have very technical, cutting-edge development of different models that will drive things away from just machine learning to wider AI. This will require researchers and post doc level teams. When you start looking at applications in business, you get more into an engineering type of environment. At this point, you require skills that look at what the problem is and how to apply the particular techniques.

Stephen Browning, Interim Challenge Director – Next Generation Services, explains:

> If you don't have a skills shortage, you don't have a sector that's growing. Once you find that you do have a glut of these skills, you know it is then old hat and waning. In marketing, personalization is where we will see the major opportunity. The scalability piece is what it allows. If we gather data on all consumers and assess it rapidly through a machine, we can get down to a segment of one. Currently, in sectors such as law, AI is used to do the grunt work. Instead of having tens of associates in the basement going through contracts of case law, AI allows you to automate it. The same is true of accountancy. Today if you are carrying out an audit, you take a sample and assume it's representative. If it doesn't show any oddities, you typically sign off a set of books for a company. With AI and large datasets you can apply rapid data and carry out continuous audits. You have knowledge of the position day by day, hour by hour, minute by minute. Management now have accurate data on the health of the company and can address issues in a very timely fashion.

Potential under-employment

The next step, in maybe 5 to 10 years, is mitigating any issues. Instead of just knowing where you are, AI can predict whether certain events will happen. Creativity still needs work. To date, it's about image processing and public datasets that people can experiment on. There will be elements of creative output in a structured, rudimentary way. A good example is generating leases where you have similar clauses; that is ripe for automation. However, we are not there yet in terms of generating something completely novel. I don't believe that complete jobs will disappear for 10 years. We may well have an under-employment risk. The shaping of the opportunities will be a piece that humans will do. Tasks will change. Humans are so engrained in working, but they will find different activities to fill their time. Different job types will emerge as we get rid of some of the grunt work. We are already seeing Legal Engineers. You need to understand the framework of the law and find services to fit that.

We will probably see convergence across insurance, accountancy and law. Each of them is about managing risk. By scale activity with AI, you have the opportunity to manage risk in a different way. Look, for example, at how many lawyers the accountancy firm EY has been hiring. The human aspects are to a large extent what holds AI back. Ethics has a large part to play. Take, for example, the likelihood that machines will replicate existing biases eg in a sexist way, as it assigns, hires and bases its decisions based on the attributes in these roles today. When we talk about the adoption of AI, we need to consider the behavioural aspects, the needs of consumers and customer acceptance. There are different demographics related to acceptance, not just age.

Innovate UK is playing a role in trying to bring ethics and the responsible use of AI into play. We will need some controls and regulation to assist not inhibit. We need frameworks that are multi-national; this is different to regulation. Our role is primarily to help innovate to drive economic growth. We support R&D which companies wouldn't be able to do alone as it may be too risky. We grant funds and provide important connectivity to accelerate business. This covers pre-start up to large multinationals. We also span many industry sectors, for example health, agriculture, mobility and infrastructure.

Lack of diversity

Policy and frameworks are also high on the agenda for Tania Peitzker, Chairwoman and Company Director of a French company called Bots as a Service (BaaS) SARL. She comments:

It is important to get a public discussion leading into actual rules and regulations. So far this has only been done in enclaves at universities, business schools and a few government-led think tanks. In nearly all cases, those participating are 95 per cent (white middle class) men who are also doing most of the speaking and publishing on policy making. That is just unacceptable in the twenty-first century as the decisions being made now on how to regulate and harness artificial intelligence in all its formats and variations cannot be left to just 50 per cent of the world's population. Women really need to get up and get involved in these AI forums even if they are not invited!

Alan Turing's prescience

As we begin our book's descent, we turn once more to one of the first commentators in Chapter 1, Greg Clark MP, The Secretary of State for Business, Energy and Industrial Strategy in the UK, who states:

> Almost 70 years ago, in July 1948, a document landed on the desk of the National Physical Laboratory in the UK, which was then, as today, the UK government's leading research lab. The title: 'Intelligent machinery'. The author: Alan Turing. It is breathtaking in its vision, confidence, intellectual fizz and prescience. Alan Turing had discovered brilliant theoretical results in logic at Cambridge. Then, during the war, in pursuit of an overwhelmingly important national mission, he had become the most brilliant and innovative code-breaker, not only building machines but also a team that continues to be legendary. At Bletchley Park, high theory merged with wires, transistors and solder to crack urgent real-world problems.
>
> Then, after the war, the National Physical Laboratory recognized the extraordinary winning combination of practical, theoretical and human intelligence in the person of Turing and set him on his future path of building machine intelligence. And here we are today, in direct descent, with a renewed understanding that the momentous potential of the AI and data revolution will bear full fruit when all of us – brilliant scientists, businesses as setters and solvers of real-world problems, investors as risk-takers, and government, as enabler, coordinator and partner, all come together.
>
> That is why I have developed the UK's Industrial Strategy, and I am very pleased that many companies and institutions have come together to define an AI Sector Deal with government – it is just the start of a deep and rich relationship, and already it has committed over £1 billion in investment. AI is at the centre of a thriving digital tech sector now worth £184 billion to the UK economy. Tech-related

investments in Britain surged nearly 90 per cent last year, more than in France, Germany and Sweden combined. A change as momentous as this needs not just sectors, industries, universities and localities to work together – as if that were not already a huge task. Government needs to ensure that the whole country understands and supports the great changes ahead.

Raising the demand for most human work

Remember for a moment the Luddites. They often come up as the group that was on the wrong side of history, dinosaurs. They were that, but they were also skilled artisans, ordinary people frightened for their future place in society. Today we know their fears were unjustified – that we have never had more demand for good, skilled jobs than when the machines have taken the grunt out of human work. And it will be the same again: AI and automation will raise the demand for the most human work; and the government, with business and educational bodies, will deliver the institutions that allow everyone to develop their skills.

It is not only as workers that some are fearful. Take our lives as consumers, for example: personalized pricing, technology designed to be addictive, our data being used against our interests. Shifting social understandings and practices – we have done this well before. Think of the way that we've been able to build popular support for stem-cell research. We are doing the same thing around the use of data and algorithms by establishing the Centre for Data Ethics and Innovation, with the goal of developing a new national consensus around data and AI.

Take just one example of what I mean. We have our mission to massively improve diagnostics with AI. Our side of the deal to achieve this is to provide funding, for sure. But even more valuable, it is to allow secure access to the resource that is our NHS data. For this, we need the public to trust that the power this unleashes will be well used to help us live longer, healthier lives.

Our democracy and institutions have the pragmatism, legitimacy and flexibility to rise to the challenge of bringing the whole country behind these momentous transformations. And this, of course, is a sense in which our task in creating this better future is in fact different from the task of optimizing an algorithm: the ultimate object and purpose is always enhancing human capabilities.

Let me come back to Alan Turing's extraordinary research proposal. When describing social intelligence, a form he does not think he can automate, he writes: 'the search for new techniques must be regarded as carried out by the human community as a whole'. The power of the AI transformation for good is immense. We, here today, bring together all the skills and functions to succeed in this most important of tasks – to search these new landscapes for the good, to echo Turing's words, of 'the human community as a whole'. Together, we will build the talent, invent the tools, solve the big problems of humanity and align all this with the public good.

How far will it go?

For answers to some of these hugely complex questions, we turn now to Professor Max Tegmark at MIT, a private research university located in Cambridge, Massachusetts, United States. His book, *Life 3.0: Being human in the age of artificial intelligence* (2017) was a major source of inspiration to me when researching and writing this book. Professor Tegmark explains:

All this amazing recent progress in AI really begs the question: How far will it go? I like to think about this question in terms of this abstract landscape of tasks, where the elevation represents how hard it is for AI to do each task at human level, and the sea level represents what AI can do today [Figure 9.1].

The sea level is rising as AI improves, so there's a kind of global warming going on here in the task landscape. And the obvious takeaway is to avoid careers at the waterfront which will soon be automated and disrupted. But there's a much bigger question as well. How high will the water end up rising? Will it eventually rise to flood everything, matching human intelligence at all tasks. This is the definition of artificial general intelligence (AGI), which has been the holy grail of AI research since its inception. By this definition, people who say, 'Ah, there will always be jobs that humans can do better than machines', are simply saying that

Figure 9.1 Landscape of human competence, from Max Tegmark's *Life 3.0* (2017)

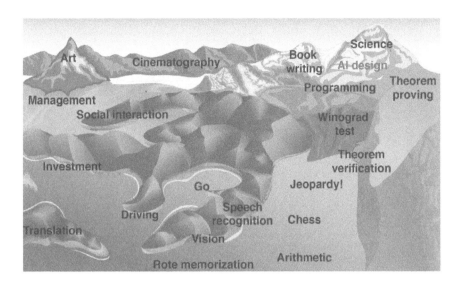

we'll never get AGI. Sure, we might still choose to have some human jobs or to give humans income and purpose with our jobs, but AGI will in any case transform life as we know it with humans no longer being the most intelligent. Now, if the water level does reach AGI, then further AI progress will be driven mainly not by humans but by AI, which means that there is a possibility that further AI progress could be way faster than the typical human research and development timescale of years, raising the controversial possibility of an intelligence explosion where recursively self-improving AI rapidly leaves human intelligence far behind, creating what's known as superintelligence.

Alright, reality check: Are we going to get AGI any time soon? Some famous AI researchers, like Rodney Brooks, think it won't happen for hundreds of years. But others, like Google DeepMind founder Demis Hassabis, are more optimistic and are working to try to make it happen much sooner. And recent surveys have shown that most AI researchers actually share Demis's optimism, expecting that we will get AGI within decades, so within the lifetime of many of us, which begs the question – and then what? What do we want the role of humans to be if machines can do everything better and cheaper than us? The way I see it, we face a choice. One option is to be complacent. We can say, 'Oh, let's just build machines that can do everything we can do and not worry about the consequences. Come on, if we build technology that makes all humans obsolete, what could possibly go wrong?' But I think that would be embarrassingly lame. I think we should be more ambitious. Let's envision a truly inspiring high-tech future and try to steer towards it. This brings us to the second part of our rocket metaphor: the steering. We're making AI more powerful, but how can we steer towards a future where AI helps humanity flourish rather than flounder? To help with this, I cofounded the Future of Life Institute. It's a small non-profit promoting beneficial technology use, and our goal is simply for the future of life to exist and to be as inspiring as possible. You know, I love technology. Technology is why today is better than the Stone Age. And I'm optimistic that we can create a really inspiring high-tech future... if – and this is a big if – we win the wisdom race – the race between the growing power of our technology and the growing wisdom with which we manage it. But this is going to require a change of strategy, because our old strategy has been learning from mistakes. We invented fire, screwed up a bunch of times – invented the fire extinguisher.

Superintelligence

Let's take a closer look at possible futures that we might choose to steer toward and consider humanity's metaphorical journey into the future. So one option that some of my AI colleagues like is to build superintelligence and keep it under human control, like an enslaved god, disconnected from the internet and used to create unimaginable technology and wealth for whoever controls it. But Lord Acton warned us that power corrupts, and absolute power corrupts absolutely, so you might worry that maybe we humans just aren't smart enough, or wise enough rather, to handle this much power. Also, aside from any moral qualms you might have about enslaving superior minds, you might worry that maybe the superintelligence could outsmart us, break out and take over. But I also have colleagues who are fine with AI taking over and even causing human extinction, as long as we feel the AIs are our worthy descendants, like our children. But how would we know that the AIs have adopted our best values and aren't just unconscious zombies tricking us into anthropomorphizing them? Also, shouldn't those people who don't want human extinction have a say in the matter, too? Now, if you didn't like either of those two high-tech options, it's important to remember that low-tech is suicide from a cosmic perspective, because if we don't go far beyond today's technology, the question isn't whether humanity is going to go extinct, merely whether we're going to get taken out by the next killer asteroid, supervolcano or some other problem that better technology could have solved.

So, how about having our cake and eating it... with AGI that's not enslaved but treats us well because its values are aligned with ours? This is the gist of what Eliezer Yudkowsky has called 'friendly AI', and if we can do this, it could be awesome. It could not only eliminate negative experiences like disease, poverty, crime and other suffering, but it could also give us the freedom to choose from a fantastic new diversity of positive experiences – basically making us the masters of our own destiny.

Robbie Stamp is CEO of Bioss International, a global network of organization and people development consultancies. He explains:

There is a real possibility that AI can help to redefine community and what it means to live in communities that feel human shaped and sized; to be able to return greater agency at human levels. But, I am not optimistic about the capacity to regulate internationally with AI. That doesn't mean we shouldn't try, but it's a much more distributed problem than nuclear weaponry for example. They are still massively difficult to produce and yes, we have them and it's very dangerous and just because we have managed to avoid their use since the Second World War, it doesn't mean we always will, but AI is a far more distributed problem. There are far more non-state actors.

I'm more interested in the deeply pragmatic daily ethics of understanding the working relationship we have with AI. I am interested in how intelligent is it? But I am more interested in asking what's the work we have given it to do? If you are putting it into the decision-making ecosystem, and you are starting to work alongside it, with it, you are effectively entrusting to it the purpose, value, strategies and tactics and ethics of your business. The point is that AI isn't human, it cannot feel, but we will – due to the way our brains work – anthropomorphize the heck out of it. To create AI that could meaningfully feel pain would seem to me to be ethically pretty dubious.

Teaching ethics

Having listened to the views of many of these esteemed academic experts – individuals who are not driven to AI due to its commercial gains – it is clear that ethics need to be at the centre of how we educate people on this subject.

With this in mind, Microsoft Corp. published a 150-page book called *The Future Computed: Artificial intelligence and its role in society*, which outlines the many advantages of AI, with advice about how to protect society from potential misuse.

This very need is echoed by Stanford University, which is at the heart of Silicon Valley. In June 2018 it announced its plans to inject ethics into its technology teaching: 'We are thinking through the ethics and impact of technological advances', comments Marc Tessier-Lavigne, Stanford's president. 'We are such important players, we should not be [teaching it] and letting society pick up the pieces' (Financial Times, 2018).

Practical takeaways checklist: top 10 tips

1 We are only scratching the surface of the moral, ethical and legal concerns posed to society and individuals by the increased use of robotics and AI.

2 We all have a moral imperative to define regulatory standards of ethics, accountability and transparency.

3 The robot revolution has the power to redefine the 'elderly', as automation can provide an immense opportunity for those who did not have the physical capability to re-enter the workforce, to take on newly available job roles.

4 We do not live in an egalitarian society where we all have access to the same resources. We need to ensure that the creation of robotics does not lead to the rich getting even more powerful.

5 Certain factors are still holding AI back. One is skill sets in the UK and globally; by this we mean the availability of data scientists and people with the experience required.

6 Ethics need to be at the centre of how we educate people on the subject of AI.

7 We will need some controls and regulation over AI that assist but do not inhibit; there is a fine balance.

8 We need frameworks that are multi-national; this is different from regulation.

9 Timeframes are difficult to predict because things could develop in different ways. Recent successes could mean that we now move really quickly with huge amounts of investment in AI, and we get so much more progress than we anticipated before. Or it could lead to inflated expectations, poor delivery and disillusionment.

10 Regulation is essential, but will everyone comply with that regulation? Consider nuclear weapons, chemical warfare, landmines. What is different is the sheer capability of AI to take us to a whole new level of engagement. It gets scary where you don't need a human in the loop; that's when regulation is crucial.

References

BBC [accessed 6 June 2018] The Big Question: Could Robots and Artificial Intelligence Do More Harm Than Good? [Online video] www.bbc.co.uk/programmes/b0b4zmxb

Financial Times [accessed 9 July 2018] Stanford to Step-Up Teaching of Ethics in Technology, 03/06 [Online] www.ft.com/content/a374fdac-6589-11e8-90c2-9563a0613e56

Jolly, J [accessed 23 July 2018] New City Watchdog Chair Warns of Danger of Big Data 'Algogracy'. Cityam, 11/07 [Online] www.cityam.com/289080/new-city-watchdog-chair-warns-danger-big-data-algogracy

Microsoft (2018) *The Future Computed: Artificial intelligence and its role in society*, Foreword by Brad Smith and Harry Shum, Microsoft Corporation, Redmond, WA

Tegmark, M (2017) *Life 3.0: Being human in the age of artificial intelligence*, Penguin UK, Harmondsworth, UK

BIBLIOGRAPHY

Abacus [accessed 9 July 2018] Why are Robots So Popular in China? 8/3 [Online] www.abacusnews.com/future-tech/why-are-robots-so-popular-china/article/2136418

Accenture [accessed 9 July 2018] Oracle Technology Vision 2017, Accenture [Online] www.accenture.com/gb-en/insight-oracle-technlogy-vision-2017#maincontent-hero

AI Business [accessed 9 July 2018] Modern AI Means A Collaborative Universe of Bots – Interview with Wells Fargo Chief Innovation Architect, 01/03 [Online] https://aibusiness.com/mike-duke-wells-fargo/

Albert™ [accessed 23 July 2018] Artificial Intelligence Marketing, Albert™ [Online] https://albert.ai/

Backholer, K [accessed 23 July 2018] We Must Ensure New Food Retail Technologies Are Pathways – Not Barriers – to Better Health. The Independent, 14/07 [Online] www.independent.co.uk/life-style/gadgets-and-tech/food-retail-technology-amazon-google-deliveroo-health-diet-a8419726.html

BBC [accessed 6 June 2018] The Big Question: Could Robots and Artificial Intelligence Do More Harm Than Good? [Online video] www.bbc.co.uk/programmes/b0b4zmxb

Chui, M, Henker, N and Miremadi, M [accessed 23 July 2018] Most of AI's Business Uses Will Be in Two Areas. Harvard Business Review, 20/07 [Online] https://hbr.org/2018/07/most-of-ais-business-uses-will-be-in-two-areas?utm_campaign=hbr&utm_source=twitter&utm_medium=social\

CNN [accessed 9 July 2018] How Quickly Can China Come Back from One-Child Policy? 13/10 [Online] https://edition.cnn.com/2016/10/13/health/china-one-child-policy-population-growth/index.html

CNN tech [accessed 9 July 2018] Microsoft: You Can Build Agile Solutions in AI in Weeks [Online] http://money.cnn.com/video/technology/2018/06/13/microsoft-ai-solutions.cnnmoney/index.html

Duke, M (2018) Why AI Hallucinates: The BotVerse Begins, 1st edn, United States of America, Global Innovation Books

Econsultancy [accessed 9 July 2018] Marketing in the Dark: Dark Data [Online] https://econsultancy.com/reports/marketing-in-the-dark-dark-data

Financial Times [accessed 9 July 2018] Stanford to Step-Up Teaching of Ethics in Technology, 03/06 [Online] www.ft.com/content/a374fdac-6589-11e8-90c2-9563a0613e56

Forbes Middle East [accessed 9 July 2018] Dubai Goes Smarter as It Embraces Blockchain and AI, 15/04 [Online] www.forbesmiddleeast.com/en/dubai-goes-smarter-as-it-embraces-blockchain-and-ai/

GovInsider [accessed 9 July 2018] Exclusive: How AI is Powering Dubai's Pursuit of Happiness, 26/04 [Online] https://govinsider.asia/smart-gov/ai-powering-dubais-pursuit-happiness/

Grace, K, Salvatier, J, Dafoe, A, Zhang, B and Evans, O [accessed 9 July 2018] When Will AI Exceed Human Performance? Evidence from AI Experts, 03/05, Arxiv.org [Online] https://arxiv.org/abs/1705.08807

Ha, T-H [accessed 8 July 2018] Bill Gates Says These Are the Two Books We Should All Read to Understand AI. Quartz, 03/06 [Online] https://qz.com/698334/bill-gates-says-these-are-the-two-books-we-should-all-read-to-understand-ai/

IBM [accessed 23 July 2018] Best Western® Hotels and Resorts and IBM Watson Advertising Introduce AI-powered Ad to Help Consumers Personalize Vacation Planning, CISION PR Newswire, 29/06 [Online] www.prnewswire.com/news-releases/best-western-hotels--resorts-and-ibm-watson-advertising-introduce-ai-powered-ad-to-help-consumers-personalize-vacation-planning-300674484.html

JLL [accessed 25 September 2018] *Workplace: Powered by human experience, 2017* [Online] http://humanexperience.jll/global-report/

Jolly, J [accessed 23 July 2018] New City Watchdog Chair Warns of Danger of Big Data 'Algogracy'. Cityam, 11/07 [Online] www.cityam.com/289080/new-city-watchdog-chair-warns-danger-big-data-algogracy

Juniper Research [accessed 12 June 2018] IoT Connections to Grow [Online] www.juniperresearch.com/press/press-releases/iot-connections-to-grow-140-to-hit-50-billion

Knight, W [accessed 23 July 2018] Inside the Chinese Lab That Plans to Rewire the World with AI. *MIT Technology Review*, 07/03 [Online] www.technologyreview.com/s/610219/inside-the-chinese-lab-that-plans-to-rewire-the-world-with-ai/

Kutschera, S [accessed 9 July 2018] Travel Statistics to Know About in 2018 and 2019. Trekksoft.com, 04/07 [Online] www.trekksoft.com/en/blog/65-travel-tourism-statistics-for-2019

Lavoie, J and Riese, J [accessed 23 July 2018] Leaders: It's OK to Not Know Everything. McKinsey [Online] www.mckinsey.com/business-functions/organization/our-insights/the-organization-blog/leaders-its-ok-to-not-know-everything

Marr, B [accessed 23 July 2018] Forbes, 20/07 [Online] www.forbes.com/sites/bernardmarr/2018/07/20/how-us-retail-giant-kroger-is-using-ai-and-robots-to-prepare-for-the-4th-industrial-revolution/#59fc69b217d6

Microsoft (2018) *The Future Computed: Artificial intelligence and its role in society*, Foreword by Brad Smith and Harry Shum, Microsoft Corporation, Redmond, WA

Oxfordreference.com [accessed 8 July 2018] Artificial Intelligence. Oxford Reference [Online] www.oxfordreference.com/view/10.1093/oi/authority.20110803095426960

PwC [accessed 17 July 2018a] AI Will Create as Many Jobs as It Displaces by Boosting Economic Growth, 17/07 [Online] www.pwc.co.uk/press-room/press-releases/AI-will-create-as-many-jobs-as-it-displaces-by-boosting-economic-growth.html

PwC [accessed 9 July 2018b] The Potential Impact of AI in the Middle East, 11/02 [Online] www.pwc.com/m1/en/publications/potential-impact-artificial-intelligence-middle-east.html

Raconteur [accessed 9 July 2018] A Glimpse of the Future of Human Resources, Raconteur [Online] www.raconteur.net/business/glimpse-of-the-future-human-resources

Skift [accessed 9 July 2018] From Novelty to Game Changer: AI and The Future of Work in the Travel Industry, 20/09 [Online] https://skift.com/2017/09/20/from-novelty-to-game-changer-ai-and-the-future-of-work-in-the-travel-industry/

Statista [accessed 12 July 2018] Global Tourism Industry – Statistics & Facts [Online] www.statista.com/topics/962/global-tourism/

Swant, M [accessed 16 July 2018] Best Western is Turning to IBM Watson's AI to Help Travelers Plan Summer Vacations. Adweek, 29/06 [Online] www.adweek.com/brand-marketing/best-western-is-turning-to-ibm-watsons-ai-to-help-travelers-plan-summer-vacations/

Tegmark, M (2017) *Life 3.0: Being human in the age of artificial intelligence*, Penguin UK, Harmondsworth, UK

The Japan Times [accessed 23 July 2018] In Breakthrough, Japanese Researchers Use AI to Identify Early Stage Stomach Cancer with High Accuracy, *The Japan Times* [Online] www.japantimes.co.jp/news/2018/07/22/national/science-health/japanese-researchers-use-ai-identify-early-stage-stomach-cancer-high-accuracy/#.W1XfvBJKgkh

The Official Portal of the UAE Government: UAE Strategy for Artificial Intelligence [accessed 9 July 2018] [Online] https://government.ae/en/about-the-uae/strategies-initiatives-and-awards/federal-governments-strategies-and-plans/uae-strategy-for-artificial-intelligence

Wadlow, T (2017) $27bn of Service Robots Will Be Sold During 2018–2020, IFR, 12/10 [Online] www.gigabitmagazine.com/ai/27bn-service-robots-will-be-sold-during-2018-2020-ifr

Wagner, M [accessed 23 July 2018] Salesforce Sprays AI to Get the Stink off Customer Service, *Light Reading*, 7/11 [Online] www.lightreading.com/enterprise-cloud/machine-learning-and-ai/salesforce-sprays-ai-to-get-the-stink-off-customer-service/d/d-id/744576

Wolverton, T [accessed 23 July 2018] A New Study Shows That Tech CEOs are Optimistic about the Future, Even If They Still Don't Understand Millennials, *Business Insider*, 22/07 [Online] http://uk.businessinsider.com/tech-ceos-kpmg-survey-optimism-fear-millennials-nationalism-cybersecurity-2018-7?r=US&IR=T/#tech-ceos-are-bullish-about-their-companies-growth-prospects-1

YesICannes [accessed 17 July 2018] McKinsey at Cannes Lions: AI Doubles Revenue Growth, 04/07 [Online] http://yesicannes.com/mckinsey-cannes-lions-ai-doubles-revenue-growth-46568

INDEX

Note: chapter references *and* 'practical takeaways' checklists are indexed as such; page numbers in *italics* indicate figures or tables